Nonna's Kitchen Chair

There Began a Lifelong Love of Food and Cooking

By

Joanne (Loiacono/Rositano) Snow

Illustrations by Terry Simmons

Photography copyright © 2021 Nonna's Kitchen Chair, LLC.
Recipe Illustrations copyright © 2021 Nonna's Kitchen Chair, LLC.

Published 2021 in the United States by Nonna's Kitchen Chair, LLC.
ISBN: 978-1-7369315-1-6
Printed in the United States

Visit Nonna's Kitchen Chair online at www.nonnaskitchenchair.com

"But when Italians say 'Mangia! Mangia!' they're not just talking about food. They're trying to get you to stay with them, to sit by them at the table for as long as possible. The meals that my family ate together- the many courses, the time in between at the table or on the mountain by the sea, the hours spent talking loudly and passionately and unyieldingly and laughing hysterically the way Neapolitans do- were designed to prolong our time together; the food was, of course, meant to nourish us, but it was also meant to satisfy, in some deeper way, our endless hunger for one another."
– Sergio Esposito

In the Beginning. . .

My earliest memories of cooking were in Nonna's kitchen at the ranch. I was four or five years old, so it was in the late 1940s. I remember I had wanted to help her cook for the longest time and, until that amazing first day, she only had me set the table and dry dishes.

But then, one day, she folded a clean flour sack dish towel, wrapped it around me, and lifted me up onto a dark oak kitchen chair at the long kitchen counter. Finally, I was close to all the wonderful cheeses lined up for grating. I had always been able to smell their wonderful aromas from down below, and she often would give me little tidbits to taste.

But suddenly, there I was—standing before chunks of various sizes and shapes of the golden pieces of heaven that she was about to put into my hands. I was ecstatic and full of pride. I wanted to learn everything Nonna would teach me, and now that I think back to nearly 70 years ago, I know that she was just as eager to use her broken English to teach her first granddaughter what she knew about cooking.

We started with her first two rules: 1) Wash your hands with soap and hot water! 2) Dry on a clean, white flour sack dish towel! Let me tell you here, that those towels were all gathered and washed later in detergent and what she called "bleaching water." The rest of us called it "bleach." They were always pure white—no stains. If they came out of the wash with stubborn stains, they were given to my grandfather or uncle to use outside (in the barn, in the garage—anywhere but in the kitchen!).

Okay, back to the cheese: we used waxed paper a lot then. Remember, we had no plastic wrap, and Reynolds Wrap was introduced around 1947—Grandma did begin buying it before the 1950s, I know, but way back when I first started my adventures in the kitchen, I only remember the white towels, waxed paper, and oh, the paper she bought from the butcher's. That was great paper too, but that's another story.

She introduced me to imported Parmigiano-Reggiano and imported Romano Pecorino. (She never used American versions of these cheeses.) She said that she preferred the stronger-smelling (and flavored) Pecorino, but there were some in the family who liked Parmigiano. Sometimes she used some of each in her cooking. Most of the time when we cooked together, especially the sugo (pasta sauce), she would throw in little bits of Romano.

Nonna's cheese grater was made by Nonno. He made lots of kitchen tools for her, including the cannoli sticks—a story I will tell you another time. The grater was a rectangular wooden box securely fitted with a piece of tin. He had punched holes into the tin with a nail in neat rows and columns. Then he glued and nailed a frame over the tin to secure it to the bottom of the box. There was a drawer fitted into the box, so that it could be removed and the grated cheese could be poured into a serving bowl later.

I still have one, and you can buy such boxes today in Italy, and perhaps in the U.S. in specialty kitchen shops. But this was a Nonno Special!

So I went to work on my first assignment with gusto. Oh, if you are worried about a young child grating cheese on such a sharp, scary device—don't. I was taught when to stop grating and put my little un-grated chunks in the appropriate pile for use later in cooking (or snacking).

Nothing ever went to waste, and we didn't cut our fingers, either.

So, what else did I learn in the beginning? Well, Nonna had me washing and pulling leaves from her fresh parsley from the garden, opening cans of tomato paste, swishing them out with fresh water and adding these ingredients to the simmering sauce, and opening her jars of home-canned tomatoes. I chopped fresh basil when she had it. And, of course, I chopped, minced, and smashed garlic, as needed.

Finally, as time passed, the chair moved to the stove. Once I could slice onions and chop garlic, I could sauté them in olive oil and add the parsley. Now I was ready for the big time! Here, My Friends, is Nonna's recipe for pasta sauce. I have her original "recipe" (she never measured anything, so I give you approximations). I learned to cook by taste, as she did, and I recommend that you do that as well. After all, it really is all about pleasing your palate and your family's.

Further on you will find recipes for vegetarian and meat sauces. I didn't eat meat for 30 years. However, my husband loves meat and likes vegetarian dishes, as well. Sometimes, I prepare both versions for the same meal, depending upon my guests' needs. You will be modifying these recipes to meet your families' needs and tastes just as I do. They are meant just as suggestions. *Buon appetito*!

Mom with My Nonna, circa 1917

Great-Grandma and Me (in her wedding dress!), circa mid-1950s

My Nonna and Me in the 1960s

And Now. . .

Here we are, 2020, in the midst of a pandemic—a challenging time in so many ways. We learn much from our grandparents and parents, sometimes about the tough times they lived through, and much about how to adapt to the changes that life presents to us.

As I pulled together the ideas and recipes for this book, I was often reminded of the many cultures and experiences I was drawing from over the many years I have been fortunate to live in such a diverse community. Even my nonna started to use some new ingredients as she discovered them when she went out to work in the local canneries, and met new friends at lunchtime who shared foods and baked treats (along with recipes).

Now too, besides just her wooden spoons and jars for measuring, we have so many sophisticated kitchen tools and appliances that make recipes more manageable today. Some recipes that took her several days with the help of other relatives, I may be able to do in half or less time because of modern equipment and available products.

As you go through these recipes, I urge you to read through the one you are choosing completely before you begin and modify it to suit your taste and needs. Not every recipe will be exactly as you like it the first time, so experiment and have fun as you go.

A word on serving sizes too: they are dependent on the appetite, age, and size of guest. So I encourage you to do as I do: always assume you need a little more. Leftovers are not a bad thing—in fact, many recipes are even better the next day!

I hope you always enjoy your adventures in the kitchen and will write to me with questions or suggestions as you read through the book. I will always welcome your feedback. Please visit us at www.nonnaskitchenchair.com

Today: Nonna's Kitchen Chair, LLC

Nonna's Kitchen Chair, LLC, bakes and sells cookies in the San Francisco Bay Area from www.nonnaskitchenchair.com. The company has just launched the first of a series of cookbooks. The next one will feature cookies and desserts!

Ken and Joanne: A foodie team for over 50 years!

"There is no sincerer love than the love of food."
– George Bernard Shaw

Table of Contents

Poultry

Meat

Vegetables

Pasta/Rice

Sauces

Desserts

Breakfast

Appetizers

Appetizers

Artichokes with Breadcrumbs, Cheese, Italian Herbs. . .

Breaded Baby Artichoke Hearts

Serves 4–6

Both Nonna and Mom used to fry these, and I did, too, when I first started cooking way back when. Alas, we try to be a little wiser today. One thing I often do is use my air fryer, but I find them easier to do in the conventional oven. You can, of course, experiment yourself and see what you think. Hope you enjoy them!

Ingredients

2 10-oz. packages frozen artichoke hearts, cooked until tender, drained, and patted dry
Juice of $\frac{1}{4}$ lemon
1 T olive oil, plus more for brushing on baking dish and drizzling over
1 T butter
3 cloves garlic, peeled and crushed
1 C plain dry breadcrumbs
$\frac{1}{3}$ C grated Parmigiano-Reggiano
$\frac{1}{4}$ C finely chopped fresh parsley
Freshly ground pepper
Salt to taste

Preheat oven to 375 degrees.

With a pastry brush, brush olive oil all around a baking dish large enough to hold all the artichokes in a single layer. Then arrange artichokes in a single layer, cut side up, over the bottom. Sprinkle with lemon juice and set the dish aside.

Preheat a nonstick saucepan over medium heat and add 1 T olive oil and 1 T butter. When melted, add garlic and breadcrumbs to lightly toast. Then add cheese, parsley, and black pepper, stirring to combine. Remove from heat and taste for seasoning, adding salt if necessary.

Top the artichokes with the breadcrumb topping and drizzle with olive oil. Bake 10 minutes or until the topping is brown and artichokes are warm.

Stuffed Mushrooms

Serves 5–6

The holidays were amazing celebrations at Nonna's, and her food was delicious and full of wonderfully good flavors of cheese, garlic, and herbs. We always looked forward to these mushroom treats. I often make them ahead of time and bake them just before serving.

Ingredients

12 2-inch mushrooms (stems removed and saved)
$^1/_2$ C plus 1 T extra-virgin olive oil
$^3/_4$ C plain dry breadcrumbs (or more, if needed)
$^1/_2$ C finely grated Pecorino Romano cheese
2 garlic cloves, minced
2 T chopped Italian parsley
2 t minced fresh thyme leaves (or dried oregano, if you prefer)
Kosher salt and freshly ground pepper

Preheat oven to 375 degrees.

Oil a baking pan and place cleaned mushroom caps, tops down, on the sheet ready to fill.

To make the filling: Finely chop half the stems (save the rest for soups or stews later). Preheat a saucepan over medium heat with 1T olive oil. Sauté the mushroom stems, breadcrumbs, garlic, and herbs. Stir in the cheese and remove from heat. You should have a soft dough. If mixture is too oily, add more crumbs and cheese. Add salt and pepper to taste.

Fill the caps on the baking pan and drizzle all the mushrooms with the $^1/_2$ cup of olive oil. Bake until mushrooms are browned but still firm (approximately 7–8 minutes). Do not overbake. If they are not browned, you may place them briefly under the broiler, but it is usually better to take them out while they are still firm.

Romaine Leaves with a Little Dip

This is a modern recipe with traditional ingredients. It seems to be loved by all the generations in our family. I feel quite chic when I serve it on endive!

Ingredients

2 T extra-virgin olive oil
1 T red wine vinegar
2 cloves garlic, minced
$^1/_2$ jalapeño, seeded, and minced
$^1/_2$ C Italian parsley, chopped
2 T chopped fresh oregano
$^1/_4$–$^1/_2$ t salt
4–6 oz. ricotta salata or queso fresco, crumbled
Leaves from 3 hearts of romaine, rinsed and spun dry (or use endive leaves)

Whisk together olive oil, vinegar, garlic, jalapeño, parsley, oregano, and salt. Stir in cheese until thoroughly combined.

Just before serving, spoon dip onto core end of romaine leaves, dividing evenly, and serve immediately. I often take this appetizer to gatherings, packing leaves and dip separately, and then arranging leaves with dip on platter at the party.

Avocados, Purple Onion, Lime, Cilantro, Pepper…

Guacamole Two Ways

Who doesn't love a ripe avocado? Give me a little salt and a spoon and I am in heaven! My great-grandmother had a huge avocado tree in her yard. It's still there at the Victorian where she lived and bears lovely fruit. Nonna sometimes would put a plate of sliced avocados out for lunch along with salami, cheese, her fresh homemade bread, and fruit. My husband would say, "What could be better?"

Ingredients

4–6 Hass avocados (depending on size), peeled and cubed (leave pit in the bowl with
      avocados)
1 C chopped tomatoes
$^1/_2$ C minced purple onion
3 T fresh lime juice
$^1/_2$–$^2/_3$ fresh cilantro, chopped
$^1/_2$–1 jalapeño, seeded and minced
Kosher salt to taste

Place avocados in large bowl with pit in the bottom. (Allegedly, the pit helps keep the dip from turning dark.) As you smoosh around the ingredients, just be careful of the pit in the bottom. I use a rubber spatula or a fork.

Add the tomatoes, onion, lime juice, cilantro, jalapeño, and salt. Taste for seasoning. You may add more lime juice, jalapeño, or salt, if needed.

There is another way of preparing this that we like equally as well, and, during the pandemic of 2020, I found myself making it more than once when I had fewer fresh ingredients around. So, sometimes, we are limited only by our imaginations, I think.

You might try leaving out the tomatoes and, instead of the jalapeño, use a small can of Ortega chopped chiles, drained. Chopped green onions are delicious in this one. Have at it!

Eggplant, Roasted Peppers, Red Onion, Basil. . .

Caponata

Serves 6–8

I prefer to use Italian eggplants, which are longer and more slender than those big common ones you see at the grocer's. It is important that they are fresh and creamy looking inside with no brown seeds. You can start with fresh red peppers and roast your own over an open gas flame or under the broiler until the skin is black. Place in brown paper bag for half an hour and remove skin before proceeding with the recipe.

Ingredients

2 lbs. Italian eggplants, cut into 1-inch cubes
3 T kosher salt, plus more
$^2/_3$ C extra-virgin olive oil
$^1/_4$ C red wine vinegar
2 t sugar
3 cloves garlic, smashed and divided
1 medium red onion, thinly sliced
$^3/_4$ C roasted red peppers, cut into strips
1 small fennel bulb, thinly sliced (or celery, if preferred)
15 pitted green olives, chopped
16-oz. can tomatoes, drained (San Marzano preferred)
3–4 T sliced fresh basil
Crushed red pepper (optional)
$^1/_3$ C lightly toasted pine nuts

Toss the eggplant cubes with 3 T of salt in a colander set over a bowl and chill for at least 3 to 4 hours. Squeeze out the eggplant in a clean kitchen towel to remove excess liquid. Rinse under running water and blot dry with paper towels. Set aside on a parchment-lined tray while you heat oven to 425°.

The recipe continues.

Line a baking sheet with parchment paper. In a bowl, toss eggplant with 4 T olive oil and spread out on a paper-lined baking sheet. Roast, turning once, until crisp and lightly browned.

In a small bowl, stir 2 t sugar into $\frac{1}{4}$ C red wine vinegar and set aside.

In a large saucepan over low heat, sauté half the garlic and onions in 3 T oil until soft (do not brown). Stir in peppers, fennel (or celery), and olives and sauté until fennel is just barely cooked (2–3 minutes).

Meanwhile, in a separate small saucepan, sauté the rest of the garlic in 2 T oil until soft. Stir in drained tomatoes and crushed red pepper, if using, and cook, stirring occasionally, until thickened. (Use a hand blender to smooth out the sauce.) Stir in the sweetened vinegar.

When the vegetables are finished cooking, stir the sauce into them and gently fold in the roasted eggplant, being as careful as possible not to smash the vegetables. Check for seasoning and add salt if needed.

Remove from the heat and stir in the basil.

Set the caponata aside for several hours to allow the flavors to meld. Then, store it in the refrigerator. It can be made several days in advance. Bring to room temperature before serving. Top with the toasted pine nuts just before serving.

Appetizer Duck Salad

This recipe serves two, but can easily be doubled or tripled. Vary the cheese as preference determines. I love dried Bing cherries, hazelnut oil, and mild flavored white wine vinegar (as opposed to balsamic) for overall balance of flavors for my taste. You may have other preferences, so go for it!

Ingredients

2 large handsful of dark mixed salad greens (include some arugula), rinsed, spun dry, and torn
  into bite-size pieces
2 T hazelnut oil
2 T white wine vinegar or Champagne vinegar
1 t Dijon mustard
$1/4$ C dried Bing cherries
1 T sugar
Sea salt to taste
1 smoked duck breast, sliced (set in freezer for a few minutes before slicing thinly)
2 ounces blue cheese or Gorgonzola
$1/4$ C hazelnuts, toasted and chopped

Place salad greens in a serving bowl. In a small saucepan, combine oil, vinegar, mustard, cherries, and sugar and cook over medium heat for 2 or 3 minutes, just until warm. Set aside.

Just before serving, pour dressing over greens and sprinkle with a little salt. Toss and plate the salad after tasting a leaf for seasoning. (Correct salt, if needed.)

Top salad with duck slices, crumbled cheese and chopped nuts.

Eggs, Mushrooms, Half-and-Half, Jack, Garlic. . .

Serves 24–26

Ingredients

For the crust:
2¼ C all-purpose flour
1 T sugar
1 t salt
½ C (1 stick) unsalted butter, cut into ½-inch cubes and chilled in the freezer for a few minutes
1½ T vegetable shortening (cold)
⅓ C ice water

Put the dry ingredients in a food processor and mix them. Add chilled butter and vegetable shortening and pulse 10 times, or until the mixture resembles small pea-size bits. Remove contents to a bowl and gently fold in ice water. I use gloved hands for this to avoid overmixing. Pat dough into a flat disk, wrap with plastic wrap, and refrigerate for 1 hour or overnight.

After dough has chilled, lightly flour a sheet of parchment and place dough on top. Lightly flour top and place another sheet of parchment on top of dough. Roll out dough, turning as you go, until you have a sheet of dough slightly larger than a half sheet pan. Keep the scraps to use around the edges to decorate or fill out the edges where needed.

Transfer the dough to a sheet pan. First, remove the top piece of parchment. If the dough is sticky, it is a bit too warm. Place the pan and dough in the freezer for a few minutes. It will stiffen slightly and make it a little easier to work with.

Next, you will need to flip it onto the sheet pan. I use the parchment sheet and, moving slowly, slide the dough carefully over and down onto the pan. Then the paper can be removed. Again, if it is sticking too much, chilling will help.

Preheat oven to 375 degrees. Chill the pan and dough in the freezer until chilled more thoroughly, 15–20 minutes. While it is chilling, begin the filling:

½ C thinly diced yellow onion
2 cloves fresh garlic, smashed
1 lb. cremini mushrooms, cleaned and sliced
1 t Italian seasoning (or 2 T fresh thyme and oregano)
2 T extra-virgin olive oil

The recipe continues.

Sauté onions and garlic in the olive oil until onions are soft, and set aside. Sauté mushrooms until liquid is absorbed and they are slightly golden on edges. Then return the onions and garlic to the pan. Sprinkle lightly with salt and stir in Italian seasoning/herbs. Set aside on a plate.

Remove crust from the freezer and crimp the edges, adding leftover refrigerated dough, where necessary, to finish the edges as you go. Prick the bottom several times with a fork.

Line the crust with foil, covering the edges of the dough as well. Fill with pie weights or uncooked beans, ensuring that the weights/beans are pressed to the edges of the foil. Bake until lightly golden—about 20 minutes. Remove the weights and foil and bake for 10 minutes more (checking to ensure that it does not burn).

Prepare the custard:

12 eggs
$1^{1}/_{4}$ C half-and-half
1 t kosher salt
$^{1}/_{4}$ t freshly ground pepper
8 oz. pepper jack cheese, shredded

Whisk the eggs in a large bowl with electric beaters. While whisking, add half-and-half, salt, and pepper. Stir in the mushroom mixture and jack cheese. Taste and correct seasoning for salt and pepper.

With a ladle, pour mixture into the prepared crust and bake until set, about 25 minutes. To serve, cut into small squares. It may be served warm or at room temperature.

Soups

Soups

Creamy Romanesco Soup

Ingredients

1 large Romanesco, chopped (at least 4 C)
1 large potato, peeled and chopped
1 yellow onion, chopped
2 cloves garlic, chopped
2 T butter
3 T extra-virgin olive oil
4 C vegetable broth
2 C milk
1 C half-and-half, divided
Kosher salt
Freshly ground pepper
2 T chopped chives

Place the Romanesco, potato, onion, and garlic in large saucepan with butter and $1^{1}/_{2}$ T oil. Heat over low heat until vegetables start to sizzle, cover the pan, and cook gently for 10 minutes. Stir once or twice until vegetables are softened. Do not allow them to brown.

Pour in the broth and bring to a boil. Pour in the milk and return to boil. Season with salt and pepper to taste and simmer for 10 minutes more, or until all vegetables are soft. Remove from heat and stir in $^{1}/_{2}$ cup of the half-and-half.

Blend all ingredients in batches in a food processor (or a Vitamix, if you have one). You can also use an immersion blender for this. Stir in the remainder of the half-and-half. Taste again for seasoning.

This may be prepared a day in advance. Refrigerate until ready to serve, when you reheat it until hot. Check once again for seasoning and sprinkle with fresh chopped chives.

Cantaloupe, Orange Juice, Honey, Yogurt. . .

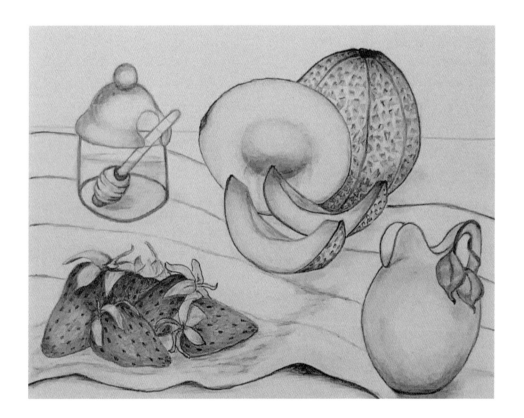

Cold Cantaloupe Soup

Ingredients

2 medium cantaloupes, rinds removed and cut into chunks
1 C fresh orange juice (or a blend with mango)
2 t lemon juice
2 t honey (orange blossom, preferably, or clover)
$\frac{1}{4}$ t cinnamon
$\frac{1}{2}$ C cream (optional)
1 C plain yogurt
Sliced strawberries

In food processor, blend cantaloupe for 10–12 seconds. Add the juices, honey, and cinnamon and process another 10–12 seconds, until smooth. (You can use an immersion blender, as well.) Add cream, if desired, for additional richness.

Pour mixture into bowl, and fold in yogurt. Refrigerate for several hours and garnish with fresh strawberries just before serving.

Peas, Celery, Parsley, Thyme, Garlic. . .

Chilled Pea Soup
(Using the Pressure Cooker!)

Serves 6

My grandmother actually used a pressure cooker way back in the 1950s. It used to scare us all whenever she used it. We would watch that little gauge rise on top of the lid, ever higher—afraid that she would be too busy or distracted to pull it off the flame in time before it blew its top! (LOL).

Now, of course, these wonderful kitchen tools, which have made a comeback in recent years, are safe and far easier to use. I use mine when I am in a hurry and want something quick and wholesome. This soup can be ready very quickly. Hope you like it!

Ingredients

3 T extra-virgin olive oil
1 medium yellow onion, thinly sliced
3–4 small celery stalks from the celery heart (including the leaves), thinly sliced
2 garlic cloves, minced
$5\frac{1}{2}$ C No-Chicken Broth (or good vegetable broth)
5 C frozen peas, thawed
$\frac{1}{4}$ C Italian parsley
1 t fresh thyme leaves (no stems)
$\frac{1}{2}$ t salt
$\frac{1}{2}$ t white pepper
$\frac{1}{2}$ C cream

Heat the oil in a 6-quart stovetop pressure cooker set over medium heat. Add onion, celery, and garlic and cook, stirring, until soft without browning. Stir in broth, peas, parsley, thyme, salt, and white pepper.

Lock the lid into place. Raise the heat to high and bring the pot to high pressure (15 psi). Once at this pressure, reduce the heat as much as you can while maintaining that pressure. It only takes 2 minutes to fully cook!

The recipe continues.

Use the quick release method to bring the pot back to normal and unlock the pot immediately. Stir in the cream and puree, using an immersion blender, until smooth. If you have a Vitamix, you can pour the soup immediately into the container and blend it smooth there.

Pour the soup into a large container and chill in the refrigerator at least 6 hours or up to 3 days. Serve it cold. It can be served in small bowls with a little crabmeat or chopped shrimp in the center. Or in small cups as a first course. It's fun to use your imagination here. Enjoy!

"One cannot think well, love well, sleep well, if one has not dined well." –
—Virginia Woolf

Squash, Carrots, Onions, Garlic, Honey, Sage. . .

Butternut Squash Soup

My nonna didn't make this soup. She often did roast this and many other squashes, and I love them all! I will say that I have had some amazing butternut squash soup in Michelin-starred restaurants. I adore this soup. I must confess, I even have made a version from scratch. Yes, I made ALL of it from scratch, including the broth, and I have whacked away at ginormous squashes as big as my head!

Today, I just don't always have the time to do that. So, here is a recipe that yields a pretty good, silky squash soup that we like. It saves a lot of time, so you can spend more time with your family and friends or doing whatever you'd rather be doing. I hope you like it.

Ingredients

I butternut squash (3 to $3\frac{1}{2}$ lbs.) cut into large 1-inch cubes. You can now buy cubes of this in clamshell containers in the produce department if you don't want to remove the tough outer peel and cut it up yourself.
3 T canola oil
Kosher salt and freshly ground pepper
2 fresh sage sprigs, broken into smaller pieces–do not crush
$1\frac{1}{2}$ C thinly sliced yellow onions
$\frac{1}{2}$ C thinly sliced carrots
6 garlic cloves, peeled and smashed
2 T honey
4 C vegetable broth (plus more if it's too thick)
Bouquet garni (Wrap 8 fresh thyme sprigs, 2 Italian parsley sprigs, 2 bay leaves, and $\frac{1}{2}$ t black peppercorns in cheesecloth and tie with string)
Crème fraîche (or whip some cream and mix with equal parts of sour cream)
Grated nutmeg

The recipe continues.

Preheat oven to 375 degrees.

In a resealable plastic bag, place 2 T oil and squash cubes with a little salt and pepper and close the bag. Toss gently around in your hands to mix oil and seasonings with the squash.

Spread seasoned squash out on baking sheet and toss sage springs in with squash. You will stir a couple of times during roasting and sage will move around, too

Roast until squash is tender and discard all sage. Set squash aside.

Warm remaining 1 T of oil in a stockpot over medium-high heat and add onions and carrots. Cook until soft. Add garlic and cook for a minute or two, then cooked squash, reducing the heat. Add broth and bouquet garni. Bring to a simmer and cook for 10 to 15 minutes until squash is soft. Remove from heat and remove the bouquet garni and stir in the honey.

Transfer the soup to a blender or Vitamix, or use an immersion blender here to puree the mixture. Add additional broth, if needed, to thin slightly. Taste it and adjust the seasoning as needed. Let it cool and refrigerate until you are ready to serve it.

Reheat the soup. If it's too thick, you can thin it with a little vegetable broth. A nice little topping is to add a small dollop of crème fraîche that has a little nutmeg whisked into it.

Salads

Salads

I love this salad, and guests do too. However, my daily go-to salad at home is the same as my nonna made every day (salad greens, olive oil, salt and pepper—sometimes vinegar, sometimes not, depending on what I'm having for dinner and how the mood strikes me). This green salad is really good, though, and I like to make it when I want something special.

Ingredients

10–12 ounces dark green romaine leaves and other mixed greens (washed and dried)
5–6 green onions (white part and a little green), sliced
2 small zucchini, peeled and sliced
1 bell pepper, cut into bite-size pieces (I prefer the orange ones)
Juice of 1 lemon
$\frac{1}{2}$ C olive oil
2 t chopped fresh oregano
1 T chopped fresh basil
1 t onion salt
$\frac{1}{2}$ t garlic salt
$\frac{1}{2}$ t celery salt
Black pepper to taste
3–4 T wine vinegar
Salt to taste

Place greens in a large salad bowl and tear into bite-size pieces. Combine all remaining ingredients except vinegar and salt and toss well. Refrigerate until ready to serve.

At serving time, splash with vinegar and salt to taste. Toss again. Taste a leaf to ensure correct seasoning before serving.

Italian Pasta Salad

Ingredients

1 lb. dry bowtie pasta (cooked, rinsed in cold water, drained)
1 small jar roasted peppers
1 small jar garlic-stuffed green olives, drained and sliced
1½ C prewashed baby spinach, torn into smaller pieces
¼ C chopped fresh basil
½–1 C grated Parmesan cheese (according to taste)

Dressing

¾ C extra-virgin olive oil
2 T white balsamic vinegar
2 T water
1 t salt
1 t sugar
2 t Italian seasoning
1–2 cloves garlic, minced
Black pepper to taste

Combine pasta, peppers, olives, spinach, basil and cheese in large bowl and toss.

Whisk together all dressing ingredients.

Toss dressing with salad just before serving.

Serves 6

Ingredients

1–1½ C cubed panettone (Slice the panettone the day before and let it dry out overnight on a cookie rack), then cut into cubes and toast in 275-degree oven until golden brown
½–⅔ C pomegranate seeds
2 Fuyu persimmons, peeled and sliced
¾ lb. torn romaine leaves and arugula
⅔ C toasted pecans
4 oz. crumbled goat cheese (optional)

Dressing

1–2 cloves garlic, smashed
½ t sugar
¾ t kosher salt
⅛ t pepper
¼ C extra-virgin olive oil

Mix first four dressing ingredients in small jar or bowl. Add oil slowly, shaking or whisking until emulsified. Set aside.

Before serving, mix dressing with pomegranate seeds and persimmons.

Just before plating, toss fruit and dressing with salad greens. Plate and sprinkle with croutons, nuts, and cheese, as preferred.

Corn, Beans, Onion, Cilantro, Limes, Pepper. . .

Corn and Black Bean Salad

<u>Ingredients</u>

6 ears fresh corn, cut from cobs and blanched (or 2 20-oz. packages frozen corn, defrosted)
2 14-oz. cans black beans, rinsed and drained
$^1/_2$ purple onion, chopped
1 C fresh cilantro, chopped
$^3/_4$ C cotija cheese or ricotta salata, crumbled
1 jalapeño, seeded, pith removed, diced
$^1/_2$ C olive oil
Zest and juice of 2 limes
1 t salt
Smoked paprika to taste

Combine and mix the first six ingredients in a large bowl.

Whisk olive oil and lime juice in a small bowl and add to other ingredients. Add salt and smoked paprika and toss. Taste for seasoning. Let stand for at least 20 minutes to allow the flavors to combine. May be served at room temperature. Taste for seasoning again just before serving.

Farro, Squash, Kale, Pecans, Maple Syrup. . .

Farro and Butternut Squash/Kale Salad with Pecans and Maple Vinaigrette

Serves 10–12

Please read this recipe all the way through before you start. I know it's not the traditional "cookbook style" of writing a recipe. However, I find the process here as important as the ingredients, and much of your success will be in figuring out what proportions work the best for you and your taste. So please change it up to meet your needs, and enjoy the journey!

This is a big recipe—one that is great for a buffet or bringing to a potluck.

Ingredients

4 C butternut squash (stem part—save the bulb for soup) cut into ½-inch cubes, tossed with 2–3 minced garlic cloves, salt, and a little olive oil, and roasted at 375 degrees until golden.

3 C farro, toasted first in a dry pan. In a large, heavy pan such as a Dutch oven, bring 8 C boiling No-Chicken Broth to a boil. Add the farro, along with the heart of a bunch of celery, a carrot, ½ onion (all cut up), a bay leaf and salt. Cook until the farro is firm, but cooked—usually 40–45 minutes. Remove all the veggies and bay leaf. Drain any excess liquid, if any remains.

3 C kale, washed, dried, stems cut off and veins removed. Tear into bite-size pieces. Before serving, rub 1T oil, squeeze of lemon juice (opt.) and 1 t of salt into the kale leaves—it makes them shiny and soft.

Roast ¾ to 1 C pecans and chop.

Snip ¼ C chives.

Chop 1 or 2 shallots (I sometimes use purple onion, depending on preference).

2–4 T imported Parmesan, freshly grated

½, ¾, or 1 C dried cranberries soaked overnight in 2 T Grand Marnier

¼ t crushed red pepper

The recipe continues.

<u>Maple vinaigrette</u>

Whisk whatever your usual ratio of vinegar to olive oil for a vinaigrette (something like 2 T vinegar to $\frac{1}{3}$ C olive oil). Then add 1–2 T of good-quality maple syrup.

Finally, toss the farro with the pecans, chives, shallots, Parmesan, cranberries, and crushed red pepper until mixed. Lightly toss in the squash (Don't mash!). Gently add some of the dressing.

Arrange the kale around the edge of a platter.

Lay out farro mixture down the center, sprinkling with additional nuts and chives. You can sprinkle a little more dressing lightly over the kale just before serving, since that doesn't have any.

Serves 6–8

I like to serve this on a buffet table where people can add their own dressing (or not) and choose what they like. Also, those who don't eat peanuts can avoid them. If you know folks love their dressing, you may want to double the recipe!

Ingredients

1 small cantaloupe
1 small honeydew melon (about the same amount as cantaloupe)
1–1$^{1}/_{2}$ lb. watermelon
2 C finely shredded green or red cabbage
12 oz. Persian cucumber (English works well, too)
12 oz. jicama
4 oz. radishes
1$^{1}/_{2}$ C seedless red grapes
1 large ripe avocado (peeled, pitted, cubed, and coated with lime juice just before serving)
2 T lime juice
1 C salted peanuts in a small dish

Cut off peels from melons, cucumbers, and jicama. Scoop seeds out of melons. Cut all of these ingredients into ½-inch cubes and arrange separately on a large platter, alternating colors. Rinse and trim radishes and slice. Rinse grapes. Arrange these on a platter, alternating colors with cabbage.

Dressing

$^{1}/_{2}$ C frozen orange juice concentrate, thawed
$^{1}/_{2}$ C mayonnaise
$^{1}/_{2}$ C sour cream
$^{1}/_{4}$ C fresh lime juice
1 t lime zest
$^{1}/_{2}$ t sugar

Whisk all ingredients together. Cover and chill. May be made a day ahead. Just before serving, add avocado to the array of other salad ingredients, and serve with a separate dish of peanuts.

Fish/Shellfish

Fish/Shellfish

Serves 4–6

Ingredients

1$^{1}/_{2}$ lbs. fish fillets, cut into serving-size pieces (I suggest striped bass,
      black cod, haddock, pollack, grouper, or hake)
6 T unsalted butter
$^{3}/_{4}$ t paprika
$^{1}/_{2}$ t kosher salt
$^{1}/_{4}$ t black pepper
$^{1}/_{4}$ t garlic powder
$^{1}/_{2}$ lemon, juiced
Cilantro or parsley (your preference)

In a small bowl whisk together the seasonings (paprika, salt, pepper, garlic powder).

Sprinkle fish on all sides with the seasoning mixture.

Heat 2 T butter in the pan over medium-high heat (not too high) and, once melted, add the fish. Cook 2 minutes and reduce the heat to low.

Flip the fish over, top with remaining 4 T butter, and cook another 3–4 minutes. Check for doneness; do not overcook.

Drizzle with fresh lemon juice and top with cilantro or parsley. Serve immediately.

Serves 4–6

Ingredients

1½ lbs. fresh fish or shellfish (e.g., sashimi-grade ahi, ono, scallops, or prawns)
½ C soy sauce
½ C honey
4 slices of fresh ginger
3 cloves garlic
4 T olive oil, divided

Mango Salsa

3 C frozen mangoes, defrosted and cut into ½-inch cubes (They are easier to cut up while they are still partially frozen)
½–1 jalapeño, seeds removed, diced (according to taste for heat!)
¼ C red or orange bell pepper, diced
¼ C purple onion, diced
1 t grated ginger
½ C cilantro leaves, chopped
Zest and juice of a small lime
⅛ t kosher salt
⅛–¼ t sugar (depending on sweetness of mangoes)

First make marinade for the fish: Whisk in a blender soy sauce, honey, ginger, garlic and 2 T olive oil until smooth. Place marinade and fish in a resealable storage bag inside a pie pan (to avoid accidents) and chill for at least 20 minutes and up to 24 hours.

Make the salsa a few hours ahead to allow the flavors to blend.

Place mangoes in a medium bowl large enough to hold all salsa ingredients. Toss in the remaining ingredients (jalapeño, bell pepper, purple onion, ginger, cilantro, lime, salt, and sugar). Taste and adjust seasoning. (This salsa recipe makes a generous amount and we love what's left over the next day. We've served it with roasted chicken and even on whole-wheat crackers!)

The recipe continues.

Heat remaining 2 T oil in a large skillet—preferably an enameled cast-iron one—over medium-high heat. When oil is hot, place fish in the skillet, saving the marinade. Sear the fish on both sides and set it aside. (For medium rare, it takes just 2 minutes per side.) However, if you like fish more cooked, place it in a warm oven after searing until it reaches the doneness you prefer.

Note: If you are using prawns, sear over medium-high heat for no more than a minute or so on a side. Remove immediately and prepare the sauce quickly.

Pour the remaining marinade in the saucepan and bring to a boil for 30 seconds, until it thickens. Strain it as you pour it into a small serving pitcher or bowl. You will have a little less than $^1/_4$ C of sauce.

Pour or spoon the sauce over the fish (or shellfish) and serve with the salsa.

"Part of the secret of success in life is to eat what you like and let the food fight it out inside."
—Mark Twain.

Crab, Celery, Onion, Carrot. . .

Crab Cakes My Way

Serves 3–4

Crab was plentiful in my childhood and not very expensive. In fact, my dad would take bounty from our vegetable gardens and fruit from the orchard to the wharfs at Santa Cruz and Monterey to barter for crabs and calamari, even sometimes for smelt.

I still remember the huge bundles of crabs wrapped in newspapers that he would unwrap on the kitchen table—some to share before we would gather around to roll up our sleeves and dig in. It was so incredibly sweet and fresh tasting.

Ingredients

8–10 oz. fresh crab meat
1 C+ crushed saltine crackers
1 small carrot, shredded (approximately $1/2$ cup)
$1/2$ small yellow onion, chopped (approximately $1/2$ cup)
1–2 pieces of celery heart with leaves, thinly sliced (approximately $1/2$ up)
1 t Italian seasoning with no salt added
1 t black pepper
1 egg
1 T mayonnaise
2 t Old Bay Seasoning, or more to taste
A little olive oil and butter for browning later

Mix all ingredients, except the olive oil and butter, gently with two forks.

To form patties: Line a ramekin the diameter of the patties you will be making (approximately 3 inches) with plastic wrap, so that extra plastic hangs over the sides. Press a small ball of the mixture gently into the lined ramekin and smooth the top. Pull the plastic over the top to seal the patty and remove it from the ramekin. Repeat with additional plastic wrap until all the mixture is used.

Refrigerate until ready to prepare for serving.

Unwrap crab cakes and fry gently in olive oil and butter in a covered pan for 3 to 4 minutes per side, just long enough for a light browning and warming. Note: I often double this recipe, and it works great.

Baked Salmon with Creamy Lemon Sauce

Serves 4–6

Ingredients

$1^1/_2$ lbs. salmon fillet, skinless, cut into 4–6 serving pieces
$1^1/_2$ T lemon juice
1 T olive oil
1 T minced garlic
2 t Dijon mustard
Kosher salt
Freshly ground pepper

Sauce

4 T unsalted butter
3 T finely chopped yellow onion
2 t minced garlic
1 t Dijon mustard
$^1/_2$ C heavy whipping cream
1 T lemon juice
2 T chopped Italian parsley

Preheat oven to 400 degrees.

Lightly oil a baking dish large enough to hold the salmon pieces and suitable for serving.

Pat the salmon dry. Combine the lemon juice, olive oil, garlic, and mustard, and rub the mixture over the salmon. Season with salt and pepper and arrange on the baking dish.

Bake for 10–12 minutes, or until the salmon is opaque. (Check the center of one of the thicker pieces.)

The recipe continues.

While the salmon is baking, melt the butter in a small saucepan over medium heat, add the onion and cook until soft, then add the garlic and cook until fragrant (an addition 20–30 seconds).

Stir in the mustard and the cream and cook until the sauce thickens slightly. Remove from the heat.

Stir in lemon juice and parsley.

Pour sauce over the salmon, mixing with the natural pan juices, and serve.

Nutty Ono

Ingredients

1 C sliced or chopped almonds, cashews, or macadamia nuts
²/₃ C fresh basil
4 C dry breadcrumbs or crackers
½ C mayonnaise
2 t Thai garlic-chili sauce
24 oz. Ono fillets cut into 6 4 oz. servings
Salt
Freshly ground pepper
Canola oil for sautéing

First, place nuts, basil, and breadcrumbs in a food processor and process until fine. Remove to a glass pie pan or plate.

In small bowl, whisk the mayonnaise and garlic-chili paste until smooth.

Season the fish with salt and pepper and completely coat on all sides with the mayonnaise/chili-paste mixture. Then press the fish into the crumb/nut mixture to coat thoroughly and set on parchment paper. I usually refrigerate the fillets until time to cook if preparing ahead (like before the guests arrive!).

Fifteen minutes before you are ready to serve, preheat the oven to 400 degrees, and remove the fish from the refrigerator.

Using an ovenproof pan, heat a small amount of oil over medium heat. (Using high heat will burn the nuts.) Cook the fillets for 2 or 3 minutes until lightly browned, then flip over.
Place in the oven for 5 minutes until cooked through and firm to the touch.

You can serve this with the mango salsa described in the Soy Glazed Fish recipe (p. 53). But I like it just the way it is!

"You don't need a silver fork to eat good food."
—Paul Prudhomme

Petrale Sole, Bread Crumbs, Lime, Olive Oil. . .

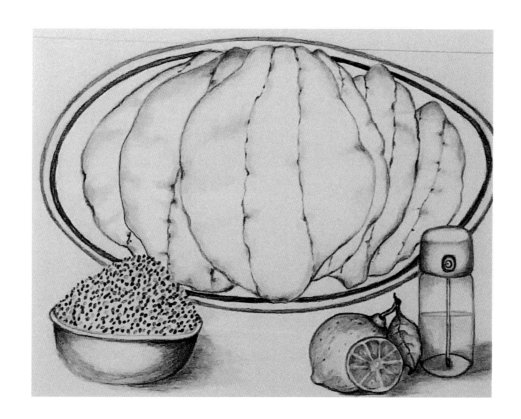

Petrale Sole in the Air Fryer

Ingredients

$1\frac{1}{2}$ C dry breadcrumbs (I use panko for this)
Pinch of crushed red pepper
Salt and pepper
$\frac{1}{4}$ t dry mustard
1T olive oil
1 lb. Petrale sole, cut into serving-size pieces
1 egg, beaten
Oil for misting (I have olive oil in a spray bottle to mist onto food. You can also use cooking spray, but it's not as good)
1 lime, sliced

Preheat the fryer to 390 degrees.

Mix the breadcrumbs, crushed red pepper, salt, pepper, dry mustard, and olive oil with fork until crumbly. Spoon onto a plate.

Dip each piece of fish into the egg and then into crumb mixture, coating evenly.

Place fish on the baking rack and cook until fish flakes easily with a fork. I usually cook for a few minutes (maybe 5 or 6, or until brown). Mist with oil, flip over, and cook on other side for another 5 or 6 minutes. You may have to experiment with time, since not all air fryers are the same. You can try one fillet as a tester and then cook the rest accordingly. Plan for a total of about 12 minutes' cooking time.

Serve on a platter garnished with lime slices.

Large Shrimp, Green Onions, Soy Sauce, Honey. . .

Shrimp with Pineapple Sauté

Serves 4

Ingredients

$^1/_2$ C Thai garlic-chili sauce
2 T soy sauce
2 T honey
1 T minced garlic
2 C frozen pineapple, thawed (reserve juice)
1 lb. large shrimp, peeled and deveined (23 per pound size will give you 5–6 per person if you are serving four people)
3 green onions, sliced
2 t cornstarch
1 T cold water
2 T olive oil

Combine garlic-chili sauce, soy sauce, honey, garlic and any residual pineapple juice and marinate the shrimp for 20 minutes. Meanwhile, slice the onions, measure cornstarch, and finish off any side dishes for dinner, such as rice. Have a measuring cup with ice and cold water set aside from which you will measure out 1 T cold water.

When ready to cook, heat the olive oil in a sauté pan and cook for 3 or 4 minutes—just until shrimp is pink and opaque. Remove the shrimp with a slotted spoon to a plate, Add the marinade to the pan.

In a small bowl combine the cornstarch with 1 T cold water and add it to the sauté pan. Simmer until thickened.

Remove the pan from the heat. Add the shrimp back to the pan along with the pineapple chunks and stir to combine. Stir in the green onion.

Lobster Two Ways

This recipe can easily be doubled if you have lots of lobster.

<u>Ingredients</u>

8 oz. lobster, cut into small pieces
2 T mayonnaise
1 t lemon juice
1 T minced celery
1 T chopped Italian parsley
1 T green onion, including some green tops
Dash hot sauce
Pinch salt
Freshly ground pepper

For the first way: 2, 3 or 4 tall stemmed glasses with slices of lemon

For the second way: "Lobstah Rolls"
Fresh long rolls
Butter, melted

For either one: In a small bowl combine mayo, lemon juice, celery, parsley, green onion, hot sauce, salt, and pepper. Gently stir in the lobster meat, and taste for seasoning.

For the cocktails, scoop the mixture into 2, 3, or 4 glasses (depending on how large you want to make them) and garnish each with a slice of lemon.

For the rolls, toast the bread *very* lightly and brush them inside with melted butter before filling. This recipe makes two lobster rolls.

"First we eat, then we do everything else."
—M.F.K. Fisher

Bay Scallops, Tomatoes, Carrots, Cheese, Rice. . .

Scallop Risotto from the Old School

Serves 6

Ingredients

2 T butter
2 T olive oil
4 cloves garlic, minced
16 oz. bay scallops, cut in half
$\frac{1}{4}$ C Italian parsley
$\frac{1}{4}$ C chopped basil
1 large yellow onion, finely chopped
$1\frac{1}{2}$ C long-grain white rice
2 C No-Chicken Broth
1 C water
$\frac{1}{2}$ t salt
$\frac{1}{4}$ t black pepper
2 stalks celery, chopped
1 C chopped, fresh tomatoes (Kumato if available, otherwise just get sweet ones)
2 medium carrots, peeled and chopped
$\frac{1}{2}$ C Parmesan cheese

Heat butter and olive oil in a 6-quart pot. (I use an enameled cast-iron pot for this.) Add garlic and sauté for 30 seconds.

Add scallops, parsley, and basil and sauté, stirring, for 3 minutes, then transfer to a plate with a slotted spoon. In the drippings, sauté the onion until limp—4 to 5 minutes.

Stir in the rice, broth, water, salt, and $\frac{1}{8}$ t pepper. Bring to a simmer and reduce to low, cooking for 10 minutes.

Add celery, tomatoes, and carrots and simmer for another 8–10 minutes, or until the rice is done. Stir in seafood mixture just to heat through. Finally, stir in the cheese and remaining pepper.

Poultry

Poultry

Baked Chicken Gone Crackers!

Ingredients

3 C buttermilk
2 t Thai garlic-chili sauce
Juice of $^1/_2$ lemon
1 small yellow onion, sliced
6 sprigs thyme
4–6 cloves garlic, smashed
Kosher salt and pepper
3 $^1/_2$–4 lbs. chicken (I prefer chicken thighs and legs, with skin and bones intact)
5 C cracker crumbs (I use $^1/_2$ Ritz and $^1/_2$ saltines)
1 C Parmesan cheese
2 t fresh thyme, chopped
1 t chopped Italian oregano (I also adore the Mexican oregano in my garden, but I think it's a little too intense for this recipe.)

In a large bowl, mix together the buttermilk, Thai garlic-chili sauce, lemon juice, onion, thyme, garlic, salt, and pepper. Add the chicken and ensure that all pieces are immersed in the milk. Cover and refrigerate for 3 to 12 hours.

Preheat oven to 400 degrees.

Mix the cracker crumbs with the Parmesan and herbs. Then set up a parchment-lined workstation with a large pan of mixed crumbs and a rack-fitted tray lined with foil. Remove chicken from the marinade, allowing excess to drip off before proceeding to the next step.

Dredge the chicken pieces through the cracker/cheese mixture, pressing onto each piece as you go. Lay each one carefully on the rack-fitted tray. Bake for 45 minutes until golden and crisp. (I recommend you check with a meat thermometer for doneness – 165 °).

Some cooks prefer to marinate the chicken without the skin, to save fat and calories. Thanks to the marinade, it will still be moist. So, if you won't miss the crispy skin, go for it!

Chicken Tagine, Nonna Style

Serves 4–6

Like my nonna's sauces, this dish always seems to taste even better the next day! So I either try to plan ahead, or I make enough for leftovers.

<u>Ingredients</u>

1 lb. Yukon Gold potatoes
$\frac{1}{2}$ C finely chopped yellow onion
3 carrots, sliced
2 C canned crushed tomatoes (I use Pomi)
3 cloves garlic, minced
$\frac{1}{2}$ C water
3 lb. chicken thighs, bone in
2 t salt
Few grinds of black pepper
Pinch of crushed red pepper (opt.)
2 T chopped Italian parsley
2 T olive oil
$\frac{1}{2}$ C frozen peas
Cooked rice or pasta (opt.)

Peel and slice the potatoes about $\frac{1}{4}$ inch thick and keep in a bowl of cold water until you are ready to use them.

Prepare all the rest of the ingredients and then assemble them when you are ready to begin cooking.

On the bottom of the tagine dish, place the onions, carrots, 3/4 cup tomatoes, garlic and water. Sprinkle with some of the salt. Place the chicken on top and season with the spices, a little more salt and some pepper. Sprinkle with chopped parsley and pour over the olive oil and the remaining tomatoes.

The recipe continues.

Cover and cook over medium-low heat for about 1 hour. Check for doneness and tenderness.

Drain the potatoes and place them in a circle on the top of the tagine. Cover and continue to cook for another 20 minutes, or until the potatoes are soft. Add peas and cook uncovered only until they are hot (5 minutes). I carefully remove the skin and bones from the chicken and return it to the dish at this point to make it easier for the guests.

Taste for seasoning. You may want to sprinkle with a little more salt, a few grinds of pepper, and a pinch of sugar if the tomatoes are a little tart. Serve with rice or pasta, if you'd like.

Serves 6–8

My nonna made meatloaf with beef. Although I often do this as well, I sometimes make it with turkey, and here is a recipe that came about during the 2020 pandemic when I made it from the ingredients I had in the freezer and pantry. It turned out to become a family favorite! Hope you enjoy it!

Ingredients

4 slices stale sourdough bread with crust removed
½ C milk
1 C diced yellow onion
½ C thinly sliced celery
1 C frozen peas
2–3 cloves garlic, minced
1 lb. ground white turkey meat
1 lb. ground dark turkey meat
1 C grated Pecorino Romano (Parmesan, if you prefer)
¼ C olive oil
1 T Italian seasoning (or oregano and thyme)
2 eggs, lightly mixed with a fork
A little tomato sauce for the top

Preheat oven to 350°.

Place bread in a pie pan and pour milk over to soak for a few minutes.

Sauté the onions and celery in 2 T olive oil until soft. Add frozen peas and garlic and toss for 2 to 3 minutes until peas thaw and garlic is soft. Remove from heat and set aside to cool.

In a large bowl, place the ground turkey. Gently squeeze the bread and discard the excess milk. Add the saturated bread to the turkey. Add grated cheese, remaining olive oil, cooked onions-garlic-pea mixture, herbs, and egg.

I use food handler gloves here to mix this gently until all the ingredients are evenly dispersed. Try to keep this light. If mixture is too wet, add a little more dry breadcrumb. If too dry, add a little more oil.

The recipe continues.

Place mixture into a large, buttered loaf pan and bake for approximately $1\frac{1}{4}$ hours.

If you have a little extra pasta sauce lying around, you can brush some on the top after 45 minutes or so, if the top is getting dry. Another option is to brush it with a little oil. My loaf is usually okay with nothing, but you decide.

Use a meat thermometer if you are unsure of doneness – 155 degrees. Some cooks check doneness by looking for the browning and sizzling coming up from around the edges.

Remove from the oven and let it set for a few minutes before serving.

"I come from a family where gravy is considered a beverage."
—Erma Bombeck

Turkey, Cranberries, Apple, Ginger, Garlic, Cheese. . .

Nonna's New Turkey Loaf

Ingredients

4 slices stale sourdough bread with crust removed
$\frac{1}{2}$ C milk
3 apples (I often use Fuji, but Granny Smith would be good, too.)
1 C frozen cranberries
1 C apple juice
$\frac{1}{2}$ C sugar
$\frac{1}{4}$ C minced fresh ginger
$\frac{1}{4}$ C olive oil
1 C diced yellow onion
8–10 cloves garlic, minced
1 lb. ground white turkey meat
1 lb. ground dark turkey meat
1 C grated Pecorino Romano (Parmesan, if you prefer)
2 eggs, lightly mixed with a fork
1 T Italian seasoning (or oregano and thyme)
A little tomato sauce for the top

Preheat oven to 350°.

Place bread in a pie pan and pour milk over to soak for a few minutes.

First, you will make a chutney: Core and slice the apples. Place them in a large saucepan over medium-low heat along with the cranberries, apple juice, sugar, and ginger and cook down until tender and all the liquid is evaporated. (If the liquid evaporates before everything is tender, add more juice if you have some, or water.) Set aside to cool. Before adding to the meat, run a fork through it and squeeze excess liquid from the mixture.

In a small saucepan, heat 1 T olive oil and sauté the onions until soft. Add garlic and cook for a few seconds and set aside.

The recipe continues.

In a large bowl, place the ground turkey. Gently squeeze the bread and discard the excess milk. Add the saturated bread to the turkey. Add grated cheese, remaining olive oil, drained apple mixture, cooked onions and garlic, egg, and herbs.

I use food handler gloves here, to mix this gently until all the ingredients are evenly dispersed. Try to keep this light. If mixture is too wet, add a little more dry breadcrumb. If too dry, add a little more oil.

Place mixture into a large, buttered loaf pan and bake for approximately $1\frac{1}{4}$ hours.

If you have a little extra pasta sauce lying around, you can brush some on the top after 45 minutes or so, if the top is getting dry. Another option is to brush with a little oil. My loaf is usually okay with nothing, but you decide.

Use a meat thermometer if you are unsure of doneness – 155 degrees. Some folks check doneness by looking for the browning and sizzling coming up from around the edges.

Remove from the oven and let set for a few minutes before serving.

"Laughter is brightest in the place where the food is."
— Irish Proverb

Duck, Onion, Carrots, Celery, Garlic, Rosemary. . .

Joanne's Duck Ragu
Using Roasted Tomato Sauce

Serves 6

<u>Ingredients</u>

4 T duck fat
6 duck legs and thighs
1 yellow onion, diced
2 medium carrots, peeled and finely diced
2 medium stalks celery, finely diced
7 cloves garlic, peeled and minced
4 slices duck bacon, finely diced
1 quart Roasted Tomato Sauce, p. 130
$^3/_4$ C Italian red wine
2 sprigs fresh rosemary
Kosher salt and freshly ground pepper
Gremolata Breadcrumbs, p. 84

Heat 2 T duck fat in a Dutch oven or enameled cast-iron pan. Cook duck until brown on all sides, approximately 10–12 minutes, and remove from pan. Allow duck to cool. Remove all skin and bones. Break meat into large pieces.

Using a clean pan, heat 2 T duck fat and cook onion, carrot, celery, garlic, and bacon until the bacon is beginning to crisp and vegetables are soft. Add the tomato sauce, wine, and rosemary and bring to a boil. Turn heat to low, cover, and simmer for one hour. Add salt and pepper to taste.

Remove the rosemary stems and return the meat to the sauce, breaking up the large pieces. Add salt and pepper to taste and simmer, uncovered, for 30 minutes, or until quite thick.

The recipe continues.

Top with gremolata.

Gremolata Breadcrumbs

Toss together:

1 C fresh breadcrumbs, toasted and coarsely ground
Zest of 2 lemons
$1^1/_2$ T finely chopped Italian parsley
Pinch of kosher salt

Nonna's Tools (cannoli sticks, mortar and pestle, ravioli roller)

Battered Cauliflower

Lobster Roll

Ossobucco

Manicotti

Cherry Pie Filling for the Freezer

Almond Cake

Fig Cookies

Sauté for Zucchini Potato Frittata

Panettone French Toast

Meat

Meat

Serves 4–8

My nonna made ossobucco ("hollow bones") with veal shanks. Traditionally, it was served along with one piece of marrow bone per person. The marrow was scooped out and enjoyed, along with the shank. It is traditionally served with gremolata sprinkled on top.

Beef shanks are a little easier to find and they tend to be less expensive than veal. We prefer the heartier flavor of beef in this dish, and so that's what I go with. Either way, they're delicious.

Ingredients

4 lbs. beef shanks, cut in 1½-inch slices
¼ C flour
Kosher salt and pepper
6 T olive oil
2 T butter
2 small carrots, chopped
1 purple onion, chopped
3 stalks celery, chopped
Leaves of 1 bunch of thyme, chopped
1 sprig rosemary
3 cloves garlic, chopped
2 C good tomato sauce (homemade or good-quality deli or canned)
2 C beef or veal stock (chicken stock works, but it's not as good)
2 C dry white wine
Zest of one orange
Grated nutmeg to taste

Gremolata

1–2 t olive oil
1 C panko
3 cloves garlic, finely minced
1 C pine nuts, toasted
2 T fresh ginger, grated
1 small bunch Italian parsley leaves, chopped
Zest of 1 lemon
1 pinch Italian seasoning
Kosher salt
Pepper

The recipe continues.

Dust the shanks with flour and season with salt and pepper. Warm 2 tablespoons of oil in a large heavy pan and brown the shanks in batches on all sides. Add more oil as needed. Remove each batch to a rimmed pan until all the pieces have been browned.

Reduce the heat to medium and scrape up any crusted meat on the bottom. Remove if it is burnt. Now, with the heat reduced, add the butter, chopped carrots, onion, celery, thyme, and rosemary. Cook, stirring regularly, until the vegetables begin to soften and turn slightly golden, 5 or 6 minutes. Add the garlic and cook about 30 seconds.

Stir in the tomato sauce, stock, wine, orange zest and nutmeg. Bring to a boil and return the shanks to the pan and ensure that they are all submerged below the liquid.

If necessary, add more stock to the liquid to cover the meat. Bring the liquid back to a boil before reducing the heat again and covering it to begin the long simmering process.

At this point, the meat needs to be braised for $1\frac{1}{2}$ to 2 hours. Some cooks like to braise it covered in the oven (at 350 degrees), and others like to do this on the stovetop—sitting on a back burner on low heat with a nice tight-fitting lid. I prefer the latter, because I find it easier to pop over and stir the pot once in a while, without having to deal with the oven racks and the potholders and all of that. It works either way.

Whichever you choose, the meat should be tender and falling from the bone when it's ready. If the pan seems dry during cooking, add more stock. At the end of cooking, taste the sauce for seasoning and adjust the seasoning as you like.

While the meat is braising, prepare the gremolata. Warm the olive oil in a medium nonstick frying pan and lightly toast the panko. Add the garlic for a few seconds, then stir in the pine nuts, ginger, parsley, lemon zest, Italian seasoning, salt, and pepper. Toss all together and taste for seasoning. Toast only until fragrant and lightly golden.

When serving, include one bone with marrow and a large spoonful of sauce with vegetables from the pan. Sprinkle each individual portion of meat with some gremolata.

Ossobucco can be cooked ahead and stored two or three days in the refrigerator. If I am not serving it the day I make it, I like to keep it in the pan, so it's easy to reheat when I'm ready to serve it. (Keep the gremolata in a separate container.) It also freezes well. The gremolata can also be made ahead and kept in an airtight container in the refrigerator for a couple of days.

Like My Nonna's Sugo with Meat

I remember watching my grandmother make this sugo when I was very young. She changed it up over the years and cut down on the amount of pork. Eventually, she went on to making sauce with smaller pieces of pork and her famous meatballs.

However, one day, the spirit moved me to try to recreate this old-time dish from memory while doing a little research into old Italian recipes online. Everybody's recipe is a little different, but the concept is the same. Brown some meat in olive oil, add some onion, a little garlic, wine, and herbs. Then add tomatoes, some water, and a bunch of basil and cook for a couple of hours. That's it!

Here's what I came up with, and you can vary it depending on your taste, since every Italian cook you talk to will have a different version of it, I'm sure! Essentially, it's meat with sauce, but usually we have it over pasta.

Ingredients

1 lb. beef chuck, cut into 2-inch pieces
1 lb. pork spareribs (meaty ones) cut apart
Salt
3–4 T extra-virgin olive oil
8 oz. Italian sausage
1 yellow onion, sliced
6 cloves garlic, peeled and left whole
2 bay leaves
1T dried Italian seasoning (or oregano and thyme)
$1\frac{1}{4}$ C red wine, divided
42 oz. crushed Italian tomatoes (I use Pomi, finely chopped)
1 small can tomato paste
Water
Bunch of basil
1 T sugar (optional, depending on sweetness of the tomatoes)

Sprinkle beef and spareribs generously with salt. Heat olive oil in a large heavy enameled cast-iron pot over medium-high heat. When oil is hot, brown all the meats, turning over to sear all sides. (I brown them one at a time, first the beef, then the ribs, then the sausage, removing each to a dish. Then stir in the onions and let them sweat (not brown). Add the garlic for a minute or two. Drain off most of the fat and remove the garlic before returning all meat to the pot with the onions, bay leaves, and Italian seasoning.

The recipe continues.

Add $^3/_4$ C wine and continue to cook until the alcohol has evaporated. Stir in the tomatoes.

Pour remaining $^1/_2$ C wine into a small cup and dissolve the tomato paste in it. Fill all three tomato cans with water and pour into the meat mixture. Stir all well.

Add bunch of basil to the top. Cover the pan and lower the heat. Cook for two hours, stirring occasionally.

Remove from the heat and, with a slotted spoon, remove the meats. Discard the sprigs of basil. Remove the bones and slice the sausages. Shred the larger pieces of meat, and return all the meat to the sauce. Stir all together.

Before serving, taste for seasoning (especially salt and pepper) and add a little sugar, if needed.

Meatballs (Polpette)

Makes 40–50 meatballs

If you want to know the difference between the cheeses Romano and Parmigiano, as well as the difference between Pecorino and just Romano, and Reggiano and just Parmigiano, I urge you to go to a good Italian deli on a little field trip sometime.

Buy yourself some good Italian bread and some small pieces of each of these cheeses. At home, preferably without a glass of wine to deaden your sense of taste, sample each one.

I suggest you start with the milder-flavored domestic, Parmigiano, and progress to the more strongly flavored Romanos—Pecorino being the strongest. Then you can decide for yourself what your preference is. It's important to know that before you start cooking with these cheeses, since they do yield very different results, I think.

Ingredients

4 slices sourdough bread, crusts removed
$^1/_2$ C milk
4 T extra-virgin olive oil
$^1/_2$ C minced yellow onion
2 cloves garlic, minced
2 lbs. ground beef chuck (you can substitute $^1/_2$ lb. ground pork for part of the beef)
$^3/_4$ C freshly grated Pecorino Romano cheese (or Parmigiano-Reggiano, if you prefer)
$^1/_2$ C chopped Italian Parsley
1 T Italian seasoning (or 2 t dried oregano, 2 t thyme)
2 eggs, whisked
Kosher salt
Black pepper
Olive oil for frying

Place bread in a pie pan and pour milk over it to soak for a few minutes.

Sauté the onions in the olive oil until soft. Add garlic and toss for 30 seconds. Remove from heat and set aside to cool.

In a large bowl, place the ground meat. Gently squeeze the bread, leaving excess milk in the soaking dish, and add the saturated bread to the meat. Add grated cheese, cooked onions, garlic, and the olive oil in the pan, herbs, and eggs. Season with salt and pepper.

The recipe continues.

I use food handler gloves here to mix this mixture gently until all the ingredients are evenly dispersed. Try to keep this light. If mixture is too wet, add a little more dry breadcrumb. If too dry, add a little more oil.

At this point, I suggest you make one meatball and fry it to check for seasoning. Heat some olive oil in a large frying pan set over medium-high heat. Roll out one meatball about $1\frac{1}{2}$ inches in diameter and brown it on all sides (6–8 minutes). Do not turn too quickly; the meatballs will stick to the pan if they are not cooked before turning. Once cooked through, taste the meatball for seasoning and then proceed to cook the rest.

Remove them to a warm oven, until all are cooked. Add to your sauce within 30 minutes of the end of the sauce's cooking time. Or, reheat already prepared sauce.

"One of the very nicest things about life is the way we must regularly stop whatever it is we are doing and devote our attention to eating."
—Luciano Pavarotti

Ribeye, Garlic, Lemon, Parsley, Olive Oil. . .

Nonna's Steak

Serves 3–4

It all started with my grandmother's wooden mortar and pestle. One of my first jobs as a little girl was getting the marinade ready for the steak. I loved this job! The fragrance of the garlic and fresh herbs brought everyone around to the kitchen, and then to the barbecue in happy anticipation of her delicious steak. We didn't need much else besides a salad and garlic bread, made from the same marinade and French bread. She would buy big crusty loaves from the local bakery for this recipe—not sourdough. It was a feast, in our opinion!

Ingredients

3–5 cloves of garlic, smashed
1 t salt
2 T chopped fresh oregano
4 T chopped Italian parsley,
A few grinds of black pepper
Pinch crushed red pepper (optional)
$\frac{1}{2}$ C olive oil
Juice of 1 lemon
$1\frac{1}{2}$ lbs. boneless ribeye steak

Place garlic and salt in a mortar and pound until a smooth paste is formed. Add the herbs, the black pepper, and crushed red pepper if you are using it, along with oil, and continue to pound. Alternatively, you can remove the garlic paste to a bowl and whisk these ingredients together. Finally, add the lemon juice, whisking and tasting for seasoning. Add more salt, if needed. (Some of the marinade may be used on cut bread to make garlic bread.)

To prep the steak, remove it from the refrigerator an hour before serving. Coat all sides with the marinade. Don't be afraid to rub it in well.

Grill over medium-high heat (3–4 minutes per side for medium-rare or use a meat thermometer to determine the correct temperature for your preference). Let rest for 10 minutes before serving. Brush with more marinade if you like. Slice against the grain and enjoy!

Chili with Black Beans AND Meat

Serves 6–8

Ingredients

2 T olive oil
1 large yellow onion, chopped
4 cloves garlic, chopped fine
2 lb. ground beef or turkey
2 T chili powder
2 T ground cumin
1 T sugar
1 t ground oregano
1 t salt
$\frac{1}{2}$ t pepper
1 pinch cayenne (optional)
1 15-oz. can diced tomatoes (I use Pomi)
2 T tomato paste
1–1$\frac{1}{2}$ C beef or chicken broth
3–4 14.5-oz. cans black beans, drained and rinsed

Garnishes: chopped cilantro, shredded cheddar or Monterey jack, chopped onions, lime wedges. Have hot sauce available for those who may want it.

Warm olive oil in a soup pot over medium heat for a couple of minutes, then cook onion for 4 or 5 minutes until soft. Add garlic and cook for 30 seconds, stirring. Add ground meat and break apart, stirring to brown it for 6 or 7 minutes.

Add chili powder, cumin, sugar, oregano, salt, pepper, and cayenne, if you are using it. Stir until combined.

Add tomatoes with their juice, tomato paste, broth, and drained beans, Stir well and bring mixture to a boil. Then reduce the heat to low and simmer gently, uncovered, for 20 to 25 minutes, stirring occasionally.

Vegetables

Vegetables

Green Bean Salad

Serves 6–8

This is a great salad to make for a party. You can prepare the beans and dressing ahead of time. Store them separately and toss together just before serving.

Ingredients

2 lbs. green beans, trimmed, cut into 1-inch pieces
1/2 C fresh orange juice
1 T orange zest
3 T white balsamic vinegar
1 t sugar
1 t coarse-grain mustard
3/4 t salt
1/2 C extra-virgin olive oil
1/2 C finely chopped purple onion
Freshly ground pepper to taste

In a large saucepan, cook beans in boiling water until just crisp tender, about 3 minutes. Rinse in cold water, drain, and refrigerate if not using immediately.

In a jar with a tight-fitting lid, shake together the orange juice and zest, vinegar, sugar, mustard, salt, oil, onion, and pepper. Set aside.

Just before serving, dress the beans with the dressing. It may be served at room temperature or chilled.

Serves 6–8

I like to have some dishes prepared ahead so that I'm not frantic trying to juggle everything all at the same time. You can cook the beans ahead, and have the other ingredients ready to toss with the beans in the pan as you warm them for serving. Easy-peasy and delicious, too. And the best part is that you can change it up to suit your taste, or to be compatible with whatever else you are serving.

My nonna cooked this way a lot, and her vegetables were often served at room temperature. She was never fussy about everything being "hot"—only certain dishes that she wanted to serve right off the stove or out of the oven. Because she always prepared a zillion dishes, we didn't see her at the table until well after we had begun the feast!

Ingredients

2 lbs. green beans, washed and cut into 1-inch pieces
Salt for cooking the beans (1T for 6 quarts of water)
5 T butter, softened
5 cloves garlic, finely minced
$^3/_4$ t salt
$^1/_4$ t freshly ground pepper
Zest of one lemon
2 t lemon juice
2 t minced thyme leaves

Cook beans in a large uncovered pot of salted water until al dente, about 5 minutes. Drain and stop the cooking with a splash of cold water. If you are not using right away, blot dry on a clean towel and store in the refrigerator until ready to use. I do this a few hours ahead of time.

You can make the herb butter ahead, as well. Stir together the butter, garlic, salt, pepper, lemon zest and juice, and thyme leaves. Make into a smooth paste, incorporating all the ingredients evenly. It helps to have the butter very soft (not melted). Roll the seasoned butter into a cylinder and wrap with plastic wrap. Refrigerate until serving time. It will keep in a sealed container for several days.

When ready to serve, warm the herb butter over low heat and add the beans, cooking them to serving temperature. Other herbs can be substituted, of course, and I sometimes add roasted sliced almonds just before serving. Play with it until you find your favorites!

"Life is a combination of magic and pasta."
—Federico Fellini

Cannellini Beans, Tomatoes, Garlic, Herbs, Olive Oil. . .

Cannellini Beans with Tomatoes and Onions

This recipe has evolved over the years and I think it is slightly different every time I make it. But I love the caramelized tomatoes and the cipollini onions, and those ingredients have remained constant. I must admit that I have actually made the dish with canned cannellini beans a couple of times when I was short on time, and even tried this with different white beans. So I have included some alternatives here. It is still good with the canned variety, if you use a good-quality brand.

By the way, I often roast the tomatoes a day ahead to save some work the day of the final preparation. And be sure to plan ahead if you are using raw beans, so you have time to soak them overnight.

<u>Ingredients</u>

1 lb. dried cannellini beans (2 C) picked over and rinsed (or 2 15-oz. cans)
$1^1/_2$ t sea salt
1 lb. cipollini onions, peeled (or a small yellow onion, thinly sliced)
3 lbs. large multicolored heirloom tomatoes, cored and halved crosswise
1 t sea salt
1 t sugar
1-2 anchovies (opt.)
$^1/_2$ C plus 2 T extra-virgin olive oil
2 T peeled and smashed garlic
1 T chopped fresh sage leaves
1 T fresh oregano
1 T fresh thyme
$^1/_4$ C white wine
$^1/_4$ C fresh basil, torn

If you are using raw beans: Cover the beans with cold water by 2 inches in a bowl and soak at room temperature overnight. Drain well in a colander.

Rinse pot with fresh water and refill it with the beans and water enough to cover the beans by about 1 inch. Bring to a boil and cook for 1 to $1^1/_2$ hours, or until tender. Stir in $1^1/_2$ t salt, and let stand uncovered. (If cooking ahead of time, let the beans cool down, strain, and store in a covered container in the refrigerator.)

The recipe continues.

If you are using canned beans: Drain the beans and rinse with cold water. Set aside in a strainer or colander. (If preparing ahead of time, store in a covered container in the refrigerator.)

To prepare the cipollini onions: While you are cooking the beans, or ahead of time, cut off the bottom root of the cipollini. Drop them into boiling water for a minute, and drain. This will loosen the skin. Now cut out and remove the center of each and peel. Blot dry, thoroughly. You may want to prepare some of the other ingredients while these are air drying further.

Roast the tomatoes while the beans are cooking, or ahead of time. (I sometimes do this a day ahead.) Put a rack in the upper third of the oven and preheat to 500°F.

Line a baking sheet with foil and oil it generously with some of the olive oil. Now gently toss the tomato halves with salt, sugar and smooshed anchovies, if you are using them. Then arrange with cut side up on the baking sheet. Roast uncovered until they are very tender, 35 minutes or so.

Slice the cipollini, and sauté them (or the sliced yellow onions) in olive oil until soft and just beginning to turn a golden brown. Add the garlic for 30 seconds along with all the herbs except the basil. Add wine and stir just until alcohol is burned off. Remove from the heat.

Stir the roasted tomatoes together with the cipollini (or onion) mixture and set aside. Bring all refrigerated ingredients to room temperature if they were prepared ahead of time.

At serving time, gently fold together the strained beans, and the tomato and cipollini mixture. Drizzle with remaining olive oil, if needed, for moisture. Sprinkle all with torn basil leaves.

Roasted Broccoli with Parmesan

There are many variations of this out there. And you can do your own thing once you begin to experiment with roasting vegetables—that's the fun of cooking, I think. My nonna roasted many vegetables, such as eggplant, artichokes, potatoes, and other root vegetables, but I don't remember her roasting broccoli or cauliflower, which I think is better than boiled or steamed. And, oh the possibilities, right? Here's one.

Ingredients

3 T olive oil, plus 1 T
$\frac{1}{2}$ t sugar
Kosher salt
$\frac{1}{4}$ t black pepper
Pinch of crushed red pepper (opt.)
1 bunch broccoli, cut into florets, then cut in half, stems peeled and sliced
4 scallions, thinly sliced
$\frac{1}{4}$ C Italian breadcrumbs, plain
4–5 cloves garlic, minced
$\frac{1}{2}$ C grated Parmesan

Preheat oven to 425°.

Line baking sheet with foil and coat with cooking spray.

In a resealable storage bag, combine olive oil, sugar, salt, pepper, and crushed red pepper, if using. Add the broccoli and shake and rub the bag to coat all of the broccoli.

Spread the vegetable in an even layer on the baking sheet and bake for 12–15 minutes, until crisp-tender and beginning to lightly char.

While broccoli is roasting, heat the additional tablespoon of olive oil in skillet. Sauté scallions until soft and beginning to turn golden. Add the breadcrumbs and lightly brown. Then sauté the garlic for 30 seconds. Remove from heat and stir in Parmesan. Add a grind or two of black pepper. And taste for salt.

When broccoli is cooked, remove to a serving dish and top with Parmesan/breadcrumb mixture.

©Nonna's Kitchen Chair, LLC

Ingredients

2¼ lb. large cauliflower
1 C. flour
1 t baking powder
1 t pepper
2 t Italian seasoning
1 t onion salt
2 T Pecorino Romano cheese
1 egg beaten
1 C milk
2 C oil (half olive oil, half vegetable oil)

Wash, trim, and break cauliflower into florets. Blanch in a pot of lightly salted boiling water for 4 to 5 minutes. Check the cauliflower, and remove from the water when it is still slightly firm. Drain immediately and immerse in ice water to stop cooking. Drain again in a colander and lay out on paper towels to further dry. You can do this in advance and chill in a covered container in the refrigerator overnight

To prepare the batter, mix the dry ingredients (flour, baking powder, pepper, Italian seasoning, onion salt, and cheese) in a large bowl. Add the egg, mixing carefully, and as much milk as needed to make a suitably thick batter. Set the batter aside to rest, covered.

Prepare your work area before beginning to fry. Set nearby a large baking sheet lined with a couple of layers of paper towels (for draining the cooked cauliflower). Have two long-handled cooking forks and a slotted spoon or basket to retrieve cooked cauliflower and small cooked pieces that float in the oil as you cook (leaving these in will eventually end up with burnt batter that lends a burnt flavor to everything). A small spoon to test for readiness of hot oil.

The recipe continues.

Pour oil into the pan to have a nice layer of oil for frying. Heat this over medium heat. To test readiness for frying, use your small spoon to drop a tiny bit of batter into the hot oil. If it bounces right up sizzling and beginning to turn golden, you are ready to go. If you start too soon, your vegetable will absorb too much oil and will not brown nicely.

Now, to practice, if you haven't fried vegetables before, you may want to try one or two at a time. Otherwise, go for five or six at a time. More than that will cool the oil down too quickly.

Dip the cauliflower into the batter and, using your two cooking forks, coat the florets completely in batter and move them to the hot oil. Turn them all around in the oil until nicely golden-brown all around, then remove them to the towel-lined baking sheet. Season with more salt, if you'd like. You can keep them warm in an oven. Or, you can serve them at room temperature, or reheat later.

Pasta/Rice

Pasta/Rice

Pasta with Fava Beans

Serves 4–6

The most time-consuming part of making this comfort food, of course, is preparing the fava beans. We try to spend some time every fava season shelling and peeling big batches of fava beans and freezing bags of them, so they are ready to go for recipes like this when appropriate.

Shelling them is just a matter of slitting the outer pod and peeling it away. To make them easy to peel, spread the beans in a single layer on a baking sheet and set in the freezer for 30 minutes (If it will be longer, place in resealable storage bag and keep frozen as we used to do).

If you defrost at room temperature (10 or 15 minutes), the skins will begin to look wrinkled, and the beans should be easy to pop from their skins once they have warmed again and softened.

<u>Ingredients</u>

$^{1}/_{2}$ C olive oil
$^{1}/_{2}$ C diced yellow onion
3–4 cloves of garlic
3 C chicken stock
1 lb. orecchiette or shell pasta
$1^{1}/_{2}$ C shelled and peeled fava beans
$1^{1}/_{2}$ T finely chopped fresh oregano (opt.)
Kosher salt
Freshly ground pepper
4 oz. (at least) grated Pecorino Romano cheese (even more if your guests love it!)
2 T chopped Italian parsley

Heat $^{1}/_{4}$ C olive oil in a large pot over medium heat and cook onion until tender. Add garlic and cook for 30 seconds, then stir in chicken stock, heating until bubbling. Cook pasta in the liquid until al dente, following package directions for cooking time. Remove the pasta from the boiling liquid with a strainer to a bowl, leaving the liquid in the pot. Set pasta aside.

Add fava beans and oregano, if using, to the liquid in the pan and simmer until tender—depending on the size of your beans, this may take 3–8 minutes. Do not overcook them, or they will become too soft.

Combine the fava bean mixture with pasta and toss. Taste and correct salt, if needed. Then ladle into bowls. Sprinkle with cheese and parsley. Pass more cheese for guests to add.

Manicotti

As with many Italian recipes, you will find that people have various opinions on brands and ingredients, and everyone thinks that theirs is the best. It's really about personal preference. Here you'll see that the amount for the tomatoes varies slightly. I happen to use Pomi tomatoes, which don't come in a can and the size is 26.5 oz. However, if you are looking for canned San Marzano tomatoes at the grocery store, the can size is more often 28 oz., so I used that size. A slight difference in size makes little difference.

Also, I like Pecorino Romano cheese, and you may prefer Parmigiano-Reggiano. Again, use what you like. Either way, use the imported cheese—it's better. In the end, it needs to please you and your guests, not me.

Ingredients

2 T extra-virgin olive oil, plus 1 T to brush on the baking sheet and baking dish
1 medium yellow onion, finely chopped
1 T minced garlic
$^1/_2$ t crushed red pepper
2 26.5–28 oz. containers diced tomatoes (Pomi or other quality canned)
$^1/_2$ t dried thyme, crushed
1 t dried oregano, crushed
1 t sugar (opt.)
1 small bay leaf
Kosher salt
Freshly ground pepper
2 T chopped fresh basil
24 oz. whole milk ricotta cheese (about 3 C)
4 oz. Pecorino Romano, grated (or Parmesan, if you prefer)
8–10 oz. whole milk mozzarella cheese, shredded
2 large eggs, lightly beaten
$^1/_4$ C chopped parsley
16 manicotti shells

Brush a baking sheet with olive oil and set aside.

The recipe continues.

In a medium saucepan, cook the onion in olive oil over medium heat until soft and just beginning to turn golden. Add garlic and cook for 30 seconds. Add crushed red pepper and tomatoes, thyme, oregano, $\frac{1}{2}$ t salt, sugar, if you are using, and bay leaf. Let the marinara sauce simmer for 15 or 20 minutes, stirring occasionally, until thickened slightly. Taste for seasoning and add salt and pepper to taste.

Remove from heat and stir in basil.

Cook the manicotti shells in a large pot of boiling salted water until slightly softened, but still firm (typically 4 to 6 minutes, depending on the brand). Use a slotted spoon to remove them from the water and place on oiled baking sheet to cool.

To make the filling, combine the ricotta cheese, one half of the grated Romano (or Parmesan), one half of the shredded mozzarella, and eggs in a bowl with the parsley. Stir to blend all ingredients well.

To prepare for filling the shells, brush a 9 by 13-inch baking dish with olive oil. Spoon half of marinara sauce over bottom of dish.

Fill the shells and place on the sauce in the prepared dish. (I use an iced teaspoon to fill the shells, because I find the long handle and small bowl convenient.) Pour remaining sauce over the shells, and top with the remainder of the mozzarella and Romano (or Parmesan).

If you are making ahead of time, you can cover and chill the manicotti until the next day.

To serve: Bake, covered with foil that has been buttered to avoid sticking, at 400° for 35 to 40 minutes or until bubbling. Remove the foil and continue to bake until the cheese begins to brown in spots. (Some cooks prefer to serve hot without browning the cheese. Whatever you choose to do, just be sure the manicotti are hot and bubbly throughout, and let them stand for 5 minutes before serving.

I do not recommend trying to keep them warm for a long period of time. The pasta will continue to cook, and you may end up with a mushy dish in the end. Gooey and juicy is good—mushy, not so good!

"If you really want to make a friend, go to someone's house and eat with him. The people who give you their food, give you their heart."
—Cesar Chavez

Rice, Apricots, Parsley, Raisins, Almonds, Cinnamon. . .

Brown Rice with Lots of Goodies

This is another recipe where you can add what you like to the brown rice, and then you can call it your own (or "pilaf," if you want). Whatever you call it, it helps to have a little crunch, a little sweet, and a little salt. So, I've given some suggestions here, but substitute whatever you like for the nut/fruit mixture. The recipe is a suggestion.

Ingredients

2 T extra-virgin olive oil
1 small yellow onion, chopped
1 C brown basmati rice
$1^3/_4$ C chicken or vegetable stock (or water)
Kosher salt

Nut and fruit mixture:

1 T butter
$^1/_4$ C golden raisins, soaked for 10 minutes in hot water and drained
2 T finely chopped dried apricots (preferably slabs)
$^1/_4$ C toasted, finely chopped almonds
$^1/_4$ t cinnamon
Dash of ground cloves
2 T finely chopped parsley

Heat the oil in a saucepan and sauté the onion until softened. Stir in the rice until coated with oil, then add the broth or water and $^1/_2$ t salt. Bring to a boil over high heat, cover and reduce heat to low. Cook until the liquid is absorbed, about 40 minutes (or according to the package instructions). Remove from the heat and let stand for 5 minutes. Fluff with a fork.

Note: I sometimes cook the rice ahead and reheat it before tossing with the nut/fruit mixture before serving.

To make the nut/fruit mixture: Melt the butter in a small saucepan, then add the fruits and nuts plus spices and parsley. Toss lightly until warm and then toss with the rice. Taste for seasoning and add salt and pepper, if needed. Turn all into a serving bowl and enjoy.

Tabbouleh

Serves 4–6

There may be as many different recipes for tabbouleh as there are cooks who prepare this dish. (That may not be too much of an exaggeration!)

Whether your ancestors came from Israel, Lebanon, Syria, or somewhere in the United States, you may have experienced a different version of this dish. Some versions call for mostly parsley and not much grain at all. Others are more grain with just a little parsley. Some are made with bulgur, and others with quinoa.

Here, you have my version. Again, I may not always make it exactly the same way every time. The main thing is to find out what you like and go with that. I like olive oil, purple onions, cilantro, and tomatoes, so I usually stick with those ingredients. And even though I love quinoa as well, I prefer bulgur in tabbouleh, so I use it here.

Ingredients

1 C bulgur
2 C boiling water
1 C seeded and chopped firm ripe tomatoes
1 C chopped purple onions or scallions with a little of the green part
$^1/_2$ C finely chopped Persian cucumber
$^1/_2$ C chopped cilantro (use parsley, if you prefer, and more, if you prefer)
2 T chopped fresh mint
$^1/_2$ C extra-virgin olive oil
2 T lime juice
Salt and freshly ground pepper

Place the bulgur in a saucepan and pour boiling water over it. Cover and set aside for 40 minutes.

While the grain is soaking, measure and chop the rest of the ingredients.

Place the soaked bulgur in a strainer, pressing with a wooden spoon to extract extra moisture and make the grain fluffier and drier. Transfer the cooled bulgur to a large bowl to cool further.

When the bulgur is cool, add all ingredients and stir to combine. Taste for seasoning and add salt and pepper to taste. Serve cold or at room temperature.

This recipe can be made ahead of time, and it improves in flavor over a couple of hours. We like it at room temperature over some crispy romaine leaves.

How to Cook and Hold Pasta for Serving Later

It sometimes is necessary to cook pasta ahead of time, so you can have everything nearly ready to serve without a lot of fuss. It might be a multi-course dinner party where you don't want to spend your entire time in the kitchen, or it might be a buffet where you would like to have most things ready ahead except for just a few last-minute items to prepare just before bringing things to the table. Whatever the reason, we all know what happens to pasta when you try to keep it warm after it's cooked—an unpleasant, unappetizing mush! There is a better way. . .

It is possible to prepare pasta ahead if you are using a good quality dried pasta. This will not work with fresh pasta, and I definitely recommend you invest in a good-quality pasta such as Barilla, De Cecco, or one of the great Italian imports. Unfortunately, with the cheap, bargain pastas at the local grocer's, we usually get what we pay for. So, don't risk it. Now on to the process.

You will be cooking the pasta ahead in a large pot of boiling salted water (six quarts of water per pound of pasta, with two to three tablespoons of salt)—that's all, nothing else added to the water.

Have a large tub of ice water ready. Cook the pasta for a couple of minutes LESS THAN the time listed on the package. In other words, you will be cooking it just until barely al dente.

Immediately drain the pasta and dump it into the ice water to cool it down immediately. Then drain it completely, removing as much excess water as possible.

Next, drizzle the pasta with a little good olive oil. Place it in a covered container. If you can vacuum-seal the pasta, even better.

You can prepare the pasta up to 24 hours ahead of time. Just before serving, add it to your sauce to finish it off and heat it through with the sauce and flavorings.

Sauces

Sauces

Roasted Tomato Sauce

Makes 1½–2 quarts

I use roasted tomato sauce in many different ways. It can be used as a base for other tomato-based sauces, in barbecue sauce, or as a topping for meatloaf. The uses are only limited by the imagination. It is very flavorful and freezes well.

Ingredients

¼ C olive oil
15 cloves garlic, peeled and crushed
4 oil-packed anchovies
¾ t crushed red pepper
2 t sugar
2 t salt
3 28-oz. boxes Pomi chopped tomatoes, with juice
6 large ripe tomatoes, peeled and quartered
1 t dried oregano

Preheat oven to 425°

In a large rectangular sheet pan that will fit across two burners, mix the olive oil, garlic, anchovies, crushed red pepper, sugar, and salt. Sauté 4–5 minutes to soften and melt the anchovies, using a wooden spoon to liquefy the anchovies. Remove from the heat.

Add the chopped and the quartered whole tomatoes, crushing with your hands as you add them, with the juice, and oregano. Mix well. Place pan in preheated oven and roast until slightly charred on top, 40–45 minutes.

Let cool and run through a food mill with medium holes to remove most of the large pieces of garlic.

If the sauce is too thick, you can thin it when you use it in your recipe. Depending on how I am using it, I may thin it with a little tomato paste mixed with water, or chicken stock. Sometimes just a little water does the trick.

Always taste for seasoning as you go along, and again when you use in your final product.

Tomato Mushroom Sauce

Makes approx. 2 quarts

Ingredients

4 28-oz. cans whole, peeled San Marzano tomatoes
$\frac{1}{2}$ C olive oil
2 medium purple onions, peeled and thinly sliced
$\frac{1}{3}$ C minced garlic
1 small can tomato paste and a little water to rinse out the can
2 bay leaves
2 sprigs of fresh basil
Kosher salt
Pepper
2 t sugar
Pinch crushed red pepper (opt.)
2 8-oz. boxes sliced mushrooms (1 white, 1 brown)
1 t dried oregano
1 t dried thyme
$\frac{3}{4}$ C chopped fresh parsley
$\frac{1}{4} - \frac{1}{2}$ C sliced fresh basil

Open cans of tomatoes and separate the tomatoes from the juice in two separate bowls. With your hands, squeeze the tomatoes gently to mash them. Set aside.

Heat oil in a large saucepan and sauté onion until soft. Add garlic and cook for 30 seconds, stirring, then add tomato juice and tomato paste. Bring to a simmer and add tomatoes. With an immersion blender, blend briefly to eliminate any remaining large pieces.

Add bay leaves, fresh basil, salt and pepper, crushed red pepper, if using, and sugar. Cook for 30 to 45 minutes, until sauce thickens slightly. Remove basil sprigs and taste for seasoning. If your sauce is too acid, you can add some honey to sweeten it.

The recipe continues.

Place the sliced mushrooms in another pan with a quarter cup of water, cooking over medium-high heat, stirring, until all the liquid is absorbed. Then add $\frac{1}{2}$ t of olive oil to coat and continue to cook until mushrooms are brown. Now add them to the sauce.

Add a little more oil to the mushroom pan and stir in the fresh and dried herbs, stirring for a few seconds until they are coated and bright green. Add them to the sauce and simmer for a few minutes more. Taste again and adjust seasoning, if needed.

This recipe makes about two quarts of sauce.

Barbecue Sauce

Makes approx. $2\frac{1}{2}$ cups

We love this sauce on all kinds of meats, such as spareribs, flank or skirt steak, even hamburgers! It takes a while to prep it (especially if you are roasting fresh garlic, too). So, I find it easier to make it ahead of time and store in a jar in the refrigerator. That way it's ready to go when we are preparing the meat. Begin cooking the meat first (marinate it or not, depending on what cut you are using), and then, when you turn the meat over, begin to baste with this silky sauce. You can always have extra on the table for folks who want more.

Ingredients

$\frac{1}{4}$ C soy sauce
$\frac{1}{4}$ C sugar
$\frac{1}{2}$ C hoisin sauce
$\frac{1}{4}$ C dry sherry
2 T grated fresh ginger
$\frac{2}{3}$ C ketchup
$\frac{1}{4}$ C unseasoned rice vinegar
4 cloves garlic, minced
2 cloves roasted garlic minced
$\frac{1}{2}$ t Chinese five-spice powder
3 green onions, minced
2 t sesame oil

In a medium saucepan, combine all ingredients except the oil. Simmer over medium-low heat for 7–8 minutes, or until sauce has slightly thickened. Remove from the heat and stir in the sesame oil. Let the sauce cool and transfer it to a covered glass container to store in the refrigerator. It will keep for a couple of weeks.

Orange Sauce

Makes approx. 1cup

My favorite use of this orange sauce is over duck. However, we have been known to use the leftover sauce on a variety of foods, such as chicken, fish, and, yes, even pancakes! Note: This recipe calls for both orange zest and grated rind. The grated rind adds a little more texture and an additional bitterness to the sauce. It is worth adding both.

Ingredients

$^1/_2$ C sugar
1 t Champagne or chardonnay vinegar
Juice of 2 oranges
$^1/_4$ C orange zest
Additional grated rind of 1 orange (use large holes on box grater)
$^1/_2$ C Grand Marnier
1 bay leaf
$^1/_2$ t fresh thyme leaves
Kosher salt
Pepper

In a saucepan, combine sugar and vinegar. Cook over medium heat until the sugar melts and begins to caramelize.

Add the orange juice, zest and grated rind, and Grand Marnier. Add the herbs, salt, and pepper and cook for 5 minutes, stirring occasionally. Remove the bay leaf. Taste and correct seasoning.

Set aside until ready to use. If used for duck, I pour some onto the serving plate, and place cooked duck over it, drizzling a little more on top.

Blackberry Sauce

Makes approx. 2 cups

Here's another fun sauce for a variety of meats. Good over duck, but also can be used on other meats. It is quick to make and stores well in a sealed container for a couple of weeks in the refrigerator.

Ingredients

3 T butter
2 T sugar
$^1/_3$ C white wine
Juice of 1 orange (about $^1/_3$ C)
1 T Champagne or chardonnay vinegar
1 T raspberry jam
2 C blackberries, plus extra for garnishing at serving time
$1^3/_4$ C chicken broth
2 t cornstarch
2 T brandy
$1^1/_2$ T maple syrup (Use a good quality maple syrup here.)

Melt 2 tablespoons of the butter in a large nonstick skillet over medium heat. Add sugar and cook until it dissolves and begins to turn an amber color, 4 to 5 minutes. Add the wine, orange juice, vinegar, and jam and bring to a boil, stirring to dissolve caramel if it is solid.

Add the berries and chicken broth and boil and cook until the sauce thickens and is reduced to about 1 cup, stirring occasionally, about 20–25 minutes. Strain through a sieve into a heavy saucepan, pressing the berries with a wooden spoon.

To thicken slightly, bring the strained sauce back to a simmer. Dissolve 2 t cornstarch in a little water and add it to the pot. Stir the sauce until thickened, then remove it from the heat.

Mix in the brandy and maple syrup. At this point, you can set the sauce aside. Cover and chill.

Just before serving time, bring the sauce to a simmer over low heat. Add the remaining tablespoon of butter and whisk until melted. Taste and season with salt and pepper. You can garnish with additional berries, if desired.

Desserts

Desserts

Nectarines, Raspberries, Lemon, Flour, Butter. . .

Nectarine and Raspberry Pie

Serves 6–8

For a light, flaky pastry, it is best to have all ingredients kept very cold. I place the butter back in the refrigerator after I cut it up, and I often keep the flour and shortening in the refrigerator or freezer after I measure it until I am ready to use it. Have the water on ice in a measuring cup and just use what you need.

Ingredients

Pastry
2½ C all-purpose flour
1 t salt
2 T sugar
1½ sticks unsalted butter, very cold, cut into ½-inch cubes
8 T vegetable shortening, very cold
6–8 T ice water

Filling
4 C nectarines, cut into ½-inch wedges
3 C raspberries
1 T lemon juice
¾ C sugar, divided
2 T quick-cooking tapioca
2 T cornstarch
¼ t salt
1 egg, beaten
1 T sugar

I use my food processor to make pie dough. Place the dry ingredients in the processor and blend them. Then add the cold butter cubes and pulse just a couple of times. Add the shortening and pulse a few more times at one second each until you have something that looks like course cornmeal.

Now remove the mixture to a large bowl. Add the ice water, one tablespoon at a time, gently tossing with forks or your hands, then turn it out onto a work surface. Form into a ball and divide into two balls. Flatten each into a 4-inch disk and refrigerate for at least 30 minutes.

The recipe continues.

Toss the nectarines and raspberries with lemon juice and $^1/_4$ C sugar in a large bowl.

Grind the tapioca to a powder in a grinder. Whisk it together with cornstarch, salt, and remaining $^1/_2$ C sugar in a small bowl. Set aside until you are ready to assemble the pie.

Roll out one disk of dough. I usually do this between a couple of sheets of parchment. You may use a lightly floured surface or a lightly floured cutting board—however you usually make your pie dough is fine. Roll it into a 13–14-inch round and fit into a 9-inch pie plate, leaving some overhang.

Place in the refrigerator while you roll out the second disk.

Roll out the second disk to a 14-inch round. Slide it onto a parchment-lined baking sheet. Cover and chill both crusts for one hour.

Preheat oven to 400° with the rack in the lower third.

Toss the cornstarch/sugar mixture with the fruit when you are ready to bring everything together. Transfer the fruit to the bottom shell.

With a fluted pastry wheel (or a pizza cutter), cut the chilled second piece of dough into ¾-inch strips. Weave these over the filling, forming a lattice. Trim them where needed, as you fold the overhang over the edges of the strips and crimp them.

Brush the lattice and edges with beaten egg and sprinkle with the 1 T sugar. Set the pie on a foil-lined rimmed baking sheet.

Bake the pie for 30 minutes. Reduce the temperature to 350°. Cover the edges of the pie with foil to prevent over-browning. Continue to bake 40–50 minutes more until the crusts are golden-brown and the filling is bubbling.

Cool the pie at room temperature on a rack for several hours.

A delicious option for this pie is to substitute one cup of plums for one cup of nectarines.

Make-Ahead Fruit Pie Filling

I started a tradition some time ago of baking stone-fruit pies during the fall and winter holidays (along with pumpkin and pecan), and they seem to be big hits with the family. In order to have sweet, succulent fruit for those pies, I make and freeze the fruit fillings during the peak of the summer fruit season. Not only is that when the fruits are the sweetest and most succulent, they usually are the most economical! So, here's the process that I follow for my do-ahead pie fillings.

Here are directions for making apricot, or peach, or cherry pie fillings. However, with slight variations, you can also do apple, blueberry, and other fillings. Once you try it, I think you will find yourself doing this more often. It is really great to have a filling or two ready to go for fresh pie when you want it.

Peach or Apricot Pie Filling

3 lbs. firm ripe peaches or apricots
$\frac{1}{2}$ C sugar
5 T tapioca flour (If you don't have it, you can grind quick-cooking tapioca into a "flour")
1 T lemon juice
$\frac{1}{2}$ t cinnamon
$\frac{1}{4}$ t salt

Cut each of the apricots lengthwise into quarters or sixths (for large ones) and discard pits. Peaches should be peeled and cut into thin wedges. You will end up with about 8 cups of fruit.

In a large bowl, gently mix the fruit with sugar, tapioca, lemon juice, cinnamon and salt. Taste for sweetness and add more sugar if desired.

Line a 9-inch pie pan with plastic wrap in two directions, add the filling, and pull wrap tightly around the filling. Place in the freezer until hard. Once the filling is hardened, you can remove it and wrap it in foil for additional protection. Place foil-wrapped frozen filling into a resealable storage bag and return it to the freezer. I have found that once it is hardened completely and foil-wrapped (wait 8 hours), I can easily stack my fillings without damaging their structure.

The recipe continues.

To bake the pie, unwrap the frozen filling and place in a 9-inch pie pan lined with an unbaked crust. Cover with a top crust, crimp edges to seal it, and cut small slits in the top crust to vent. Place on a foil-lined baking sheet and bake at 375° until crust is browned and filling is bubbling, $1\frac{1}{4}$–$1\frac{1}{2}$ hours. Midway through, cover the outer edges of the crust with a loose ring of foil to keep it from over-browning.

Cherry Pie Filling

5 C pitted fresh cherries (I prefer Bing cherries)
$\frac{3}{4}$ C sugar
2 T cornstarch
2 T tapioca flour
1 T lemon juice
$\frac{1}{2}$ t almond extract
$\frac{1}{4}$ t salt

Mix the pitted cherries with the sugar, cornstarch, tapioca flour, lemon juice, almond extract, and salt. Set aside for 15–20 minutes. Stir together again, thoroughly.

Meanwhile, line a 9-inch pie plate with plastic wrap in two directions. Once the filling has rested, pour the filling into the lined plate, and pull the wrapping around tightly. Place in the freezer overnight or for at least 6–8 hours.

When it is frozen solid, remove the plastic wrap and rewrap the filling completely in plastic wrap. (I usually add another layer of aluminum foil to help protect the pie filling in the freezer.) Then, place the wrapped filling in a freezer bag and store in the freezer until ready to use.

Small Berry Crisp

So, do you sometimes wish that dessert recipes weren't so big? It seems like I am always giving away or freezing half a dessert, because the bounty is just too much for us to consume in a day or two. On one of those occasions when I really didn't have all that many berries and I didn't need a huge dessert, I came up with this one, and now this is the way I usually make it!

Ingredients

1½ C + 2 T quick cooking old fashioned oats
¾ C all-purpose flour
½ C golden brown sugar
½ t salt
1 stick cold butter, diced
1½ C raspberries
1½ C blackberries
¼ C sugar
1 T orange juice
1 t vanilla extract
2 T flour

Preheat oven to 350°.

Butter a small, 7 x 9-inch pan and set it aside.

In a medium bowl, mix the oats, flour, sugar and salt. Then, with your hands or a pastry cutter, mix in the butter until the mixture forms crumbs.

Place the berries in another bowl with the sugar, orange juice, and vanilla. Stir together and toss with the 1 T flour.

Place the berry mixture in the prepared pan. Sprinkle the oat mixture evenly over the top. Bake for about 30 minutes or until the top is golden and berries are bubbly. Serve warm.

If you are storing leftovers, cover with plastic wrap and store in the refrigerator for up to two or three days.

Serves 4

Ingredients

6 oz. dark chocolate, chopped
3 eggs, separated and brought to room temperature
2 T light rum
$\frac{1}{4}$ t almond extract
$\frac{1}{4}$ t ground nutmeg
Whipped cream

Melt the chocolate in a bowl over simmering water. Remove from heat. Beat egg yolks until thick and lemon-colored. Stir a little warm chocolate into the egg yolks. Then, add all the yolks to the chocolate, stirring well. Stir in the rum, almond extract, and nutmeg.

Beat the egg whites until stiff peaks form. Gently fold them into the chocolate mixture. Spoon the mixture into small serving stemmed glasses or dessert cups. Chill.

At serving time, garnish with whipped cream.

Almond Cake

Ingredients

3 large eggs
$^3/_4$ C sugar
$^1/_2$ C plus 1 T extra-virgin olive oil
$^1/_2$ t vanilla extract
$^1/_4$ t almond extract
Zest of $^1/_2$ medium orange
$^1/_4$ C orange juice
$^1/_4$ C Grand Marnier (opt) If you don't use it, substitute an additional $^1/_4$ C orange juice)
1 C all-purpose flour
$^1/_2$ C almond flour
$1^1/_2$ t baking powder
1 t kosher salt

Glaze

1 C confectioners' sugar
3 T milk
2 T unsalted butter, softened
A few drops fresh orange juice
$1–1^1/_2$ C sliced almonds, toasted and cooled

Preheat oven to 350°.

Butter and flour a 9-inch round springform pan and set it aside.

Crack the eggs into a large mixing bowl and whisk them lightly. Add the sugar and whisk for about 30 seconds. Add the olive oil and whisk until the mixture is lighter in color and thickened slightly, about 45 seconds. Whisk in the extracts and zest, followed by the juice and Grand Marnier, if you are using.

Add the dry ingredients to the bowl and whisk until thoroughly combined. Continue whisking until smooth, about 30 seconds more.

Pour the batter into the prepared pan and bake for 30 to 45 minutes. (Times will vary, depending on oven temperatures.) Rotate about halfway through baking. It is done when it begins to pull away from the sides and springs back lightly when touched. Cake tester should come out clean when inserted in center.

The recipe continues.

Allow the cake to cool in the pan for 10 minutes before gently removing it from the pan and letting it cool completely on a rack.

While it is cooling, prepare the glaze. Sift the confectioner's sugar into a medium bowl. Whisk in the milk until completely smooth and then whisk in the butter. Taste the glaze for sweetness and add a little orange juice to balance the flavor if needed. Stir in the toasted almonds.

Place the cake on a small piece of parchment on a rack with foil underneath to allow for easy cleanup. Begin the glazing at the top, covering the top and sides as evenly and completely as possible. I like a nice coverage, so I use lots of almonds for this. I use a smaller spatula on the sides and sometimes my gloved fingers to finish off the last almonds on the sides.

When satisfied, you are ready to carefully transfer the cake to a serving plate.

My Nonna's Cream Puffs

(Using Today's Tools!)

First of all, I need to tell you that my grandmother used only a wooden spoon to prepare the pastry for her delightful clouds of pastry. They were perfection. None of us in the family could ever duplicate them using just a wooden spoon. I am certain there are skilled pastry chefs out there who can.

I found that I can make lovely cream puffs and little pâte à choux appetizers perfectly with the same ingredients—which, by the way, appear to be the same ingredients I found online just about everywhere cream puffs and pâte à choux were featured. So, the ratio of flour to butter and sugar/salt is all the same. What really matters, I think, is how you handle it from there. So, here we go!

Ingredients

1 C hot water
½ C butter
1 T sugar
½ t salt
1 C sifted flour
4 eggs (I crack them open ahead of time, each in its own dish—ready to add)

Preheat oven to 450 degrees. (If your oven runs hot, you may choose a lower temp and bake longer.)

Bring water, butter, salt, and sugar to a boil in small, heavy saucepan. Add sifted flour and beat vigorously with a wooden spoon, per Nonna (or use an electric hand whisk) until the mixture leaves the sides of the pan.

Remove from the heat. I place the mixture in the bowl of my stand mixer and let it cool slightly. Using the paddle attachment, at medium speed, add one egg at a time, beating well after each addition, until mixture has a smooth, glossy finish.

The recipe continues.

Drop by spoonful onto a baking sheet (line with parchment if you'd like), two inches apart, or you can bake in greased muffin tins. If using the latter, butter and spray pans with nonstick cooking spray first, and after cooking, let the tins cool a little before attempting to remove the puffs.

Bake 15–20 minutes until golden. While still hot, immediately poke a small hole in the side of each puff with a wooden pick to let steam escape. Cool on racks. Slice open and fill just before serving with sweetened whipping cream, vanilla custard, or a little of both. Sprinkle lightly with powdered sugar.

Vanilla Custard

1 C sugar
$^1/_2$ C flour
$^1/_4$ t salt
3 C milk
4 egg yolks
3 T unsalted butter
$1^1/_2$ t vanilla extract (I use double strength extract)

Whisk together sugar, flour, and salt in a saucepan. Over moderate heat, stir in milk gradually until mixture is thick and bubbling. Lower heat, continuing to stir for 2 minutes. Remove from heat.

In a small bowl containing the egg yolks, add a small amount of the warm milk mixture to eggs as you cream them, then gradually add the rest of milk mixture. Return all of the mixture to saucepan and bring gently to boil for 2 minutes more. Add the butter and vanilla, stirring to combine. Transfer the custard to a shallow bowl to cool, placing plastic wrap on top to prevent a skin from forming. Refrigerate to cool completely.

Cannoli Filling

If you you've talked to a few Italian cooks about cannoli, you already know that there are probably nearly as many cannoli recipes as there are Italian chefs in America! As with just about anything else, people like what they like and that's the way it should be. Our tastes evolve over time and they begin developing when we are infants. We have new experiences and try new things as we grow. Well, you know the rest.

I'm including here a basic filling recipe and offering a couple of suggestions. We buy our shells at a local Italian market or deli. I recommend that you do the same, unless you really want to try your hand at making your own. I learned how from my nonna, who used handmade wooden cannoli sticks made for her by my nonno. However, it used to take me a day just to make all the shells. Now, we buy nice ones from good purveyors.

I sometimes serve cannoli filling with fresh fruit in the summertime as a light luncheon dessert. I have a friend who serves it in ice cream cones topped with shaved chocolate. If you are going to fill cannoli shells, I recommend that you wait to fill them until just before serving, to keep them crisp. Top with powdered sugar and add a piece of candied orange, a sliver of chocolate, or a piece of pistachio on each end to decorate.

Ingredients for 24 cannoli

2 lbs. whole milk ricotta
$1\frac{1}{2}$ C sugar
$1\frac{1}{2}$ T vanilla extract
$\frac{1}{2}$ C grated chocolate or chocolate chips
$\frac{3}{4}$ C chopped citron (opt.—for cannoli, not for fruit salad or ice cream cones)
Candied orange, chopped pistachios, slivers of chocolate for garnish
Powdered sugar for dusting cannoli

Press the ricotta through a fine mesh strainer into a large bowl. Stir in the sugar and vanilla, and refrigerate overnight.

When ready to serve the cannoli, stir in the chocolate and the citron if you are using it. Use a pastry bag to fill the cannoli. Decorate the ends and sprinkle with powdered sugar.

If you are using the filling for a fruit compote, you can use the chocolate or not. Add other ingredients as preferred, depending on what fruit you are topping. I think it's good just as it is with just a little candied orange, but you serve it the way you like.

Pineapple, Nectarines, Rum, Honey, Ginger, Limes. . .

Grilled Fruit with Rum Glaze

<u>Ingredients</u>

1 C rum (preferably dark rum)
1 C honey (preferably clover honey, or another mild-flavored variety)
6 slices fresh ginger
$\frac{1}{4}$ C fresh lime juice
1 medium pineapple
8–10 ripe nectarines

In a small saucepan heat rum, honey, and ginger over medium heat until reduced by half. Remove from heat and stir in the lime juice. Refrigerate until serving time and remove the ginger beforehand.

Prepare the fruit just before grilling.

Remove the core from the pineapple. Slice the pineapple in half vertically. Then slice each half in thirds, so you have six pieces with the outside shell remaining on each slice.

If you have help with this, you can proceed with brushing some of the glaze on each of the pineapple pieces and grill on both sides. Depending on how hot the grill is, it takes 6–8 minutes. While it's grilling, your helpers can be preparing the nectarines. If you don't have help, I recommend that you prepare all of the fruit in advance of beginning to grill.

Halve the nectarines and remove the pits. Brush with the glaze just before grilling. Grill cut side down until lightly charred but still firm. This usually takes 6 or 7 minutes, depending, again, on the heat of your grill. Do not overcook!

Arrange slices of grilled fruit on a platter for self-serving or arrange small pieces of fruit in compotes with vanilla ice cream for an extra special treat!

Fig Cookies

Makes 24

I bought something like this at a street market once, and I had to figure out how to make them. I make a soft dough, roll it thin, and spread it with a soft fig paste with a hint of orange. To make it a little easier on myself, I make the dough the day before and steam the figs in the morning.

Pastry:

$1^1/_2$ lbs. flour
1 T baking powder
$^1/_2$ t salt
$^1/_3$ C sugar
$^2/_3$ C milk
$1^1/_4$ t vanilla extract (I let it overflow the measuring spoon a little)
2 eggs, beaten
6 oz. cold, unsalted butter, cut into ½-inch cubes and kept cold
6 oz. cold vegetable shortening (substitute $^1/_4$ C lard if you use it)

Filling

1 lb. black figs, stems removed
1–2 T orange marmalade
1 T honey
1 T orange zest
1–2 T water, as needed
1 large egg, beaten

In a food processor mix the flour, baking powder, salt, and sugar. In a separate bowl, mix the milk, vanilla, and eggs. Set aside.

Add the butter cubes to the flour mixture in the food processor, and pulse a few times for one second each. Then add the cold shortening or lard. Pulse for one second each until it's a crumbly mixture with small pea-size pieces.

Remove the mixture to a large bowl and add the egg/milk/vanilla mixture. Mix lightly with a wooden spoon or spatula until a soft dough form and finish forming with your hands into a ball. On parchment paper on the work surface, cut ball into four pieces.

The recipe continues.

Flatten each piece into a small rectangular disk, and wrap each with plastic wrap. Refrigerate for at least 30 minutes, until you are ready to roll it out and form the cookies.

For the filling, steam the figs in a strainer over simmering water until they are very soft. Remove to a colander to drain, and dry further with towels.

In a food processor place figs in batches and process until you have a paste. Add the honey, marmalade, and zest to taste—too much orange will mask the flavor of the figs, so a little goes a long way here. Add enough water to make a smooth paste.

Preheat oven to 350°.

To assemble the cookies: Remove the disks from the refrigerator. You may want to start with two, so that they don't get too soft before you get to them. If you find the dough is getting too soft to work with, return it to the refrigerator to chill again before proceeding.

On a floured parchment, with parchment on top, flour the top and roll the disk into a 10 x 14-inch rectangle (about $\frac{1}{8}$ inch thick). Spread $\frac{1}{2}$ C of the fig mixture across half of the surface along the long side, pressing it in as you go. Fold the other half over the filling and crimp the edges all around. Smooth the top as you go.

Brush the top with some of the beaten egg and cut slits in the top to let the steam escape. I cut the slits where I'm going to break the cookies after baking. So, assuming your package is 14 inches, and you want 6 cookies, you will want approximately 5 slits in the piece.

Follow this same procedure with the remaining dough. Bake for 18 minutes, until the packages are golden-brown. Remove from the oven and let cool on a rack. Break or cut apart at the slits.

We like these as they are, while some cooks like them with a frosting. If you decide to frost them, here is a simple icing for warm cookies:

1 C confectioner's sugar
$\frac{1}{2}$ t vanilla extract
$1\frac{1}{2}$ –2 T orange juice

In a small bowl mix the vanilla into the sugar first. Then whisk in the orange juice until you have a smooth, thin icing that you can spread over the warm cookies.

Breakfast

Breakfast

Eggs, Milk, Cheese, Onion, Vegetables, Basil. . .

Zucchini Potato Frittata

Serves 4–6

Ingredients

8 eggs
$^3/_4$ t dried herbs (I use a good quality Italian seasoning)
$^1/_4$ C grated Pecorino Romano cheese (or Parmesan, if you prefer)
3 T half-and-half or whole milk
3–4 T olive oil
Several slices of boiled potato
1 small zucchini, cooked and sliced
$^1/_2$ C lightly sautéed yellow onion
1 C chopped cooked spinach (drained and squeezed before chopping)
Salt and freshly ground pepper to taste
Fresh basil and extra grated cheese for garnish

Preheat oven to 350°.

In a bowl, beat eggs with salt, herbs, cheese, and half-and-half and set aside. I prefer a good Pecorino Romano, but many Americans, I think, prefer Parmesan. It's really a matter of personal taste, so choose what you like and go for it.

Pour olive oil into a 10- or 12-inch skillet, then add the sliced potatoes and zucchini in one layer, heating over low heat until most of the oil is absorbed and the vegetables have browned a bit. Season with pepper. Sprinkle the onion all around and poke the spinach in between the vegetables with a chopstick so that it will peek through when the frittata is flipped over. Turn the heat very low, and continue cooking until all ingredients are hot.

Pour egg mixture slowly around the edges of pan first, ending in the center.

Place the pan in the oven and bake for 10–15 minutes until the eggs puff up and are completely set. Watch it carefully, so that it doesn't overcook and the eggs become too dry. When set, remove from the oven and flip onto a serving plate to serve.

The recipe continues.

A couple of notes to save time: I usually cook extra vegetables whenever I cook them, because I use them in so many ways later. However, if you are ready to make a frittata and don't have cooked asparagus or zucchini, you can prep them and pop them into the microwave with a little water for a minute or two. Drain thoroughly on paper towels and they will be ready to go.

I often cook my spinach in olive oil with garlic, which will add additional flavor to the frittata later.

And one more thing, before I forget: We LOVE leftover frittata the next day!

Pear Frittata

Ingredients

2 firm ripe pears, peeled, cored, and chopped into ½-inch chunks (to prevent browning, keep
     the cut pears in a bowl with a little Ball Fruit-Fresh and water as you work)
2 T butter
6 large eggs
½ C milk
¼ C all-purpose flour
1 T sugar
1¼ t vanilla extract
¼ t salt

Topping

1½ C whipped mascarpone (add a little cream, if needed to whip)
2 T firmly packed brown sugar

Preheat oven to 425°. Drain the pears and towel dry before proceeding.

In a 9- or 10-inch ovenproof nonstick skillet, melt the butter over medium heat. Add the pears and cook until lightly browned, 6 or 7 minutes. Remove from heat.

In a bowl, whisk together the eggs, milk, flour, sugar, vanilla, and salt. Pour the egg mixture over the pears, beginning around the outside edges and ending in the center.

Bake until the frittata is lightly golden and set in the center, 8 to 12 minutes.

Cut into wedges and spoon dollops of mascarpone on each serving. Sprinkle with brown sugar.

Upside-Down French Toast with Pineapple

Serves 4–6

For a special breakfast or brunch, this one is a showstopper. The good news is that you can do most of the prep work the night before, and spend your time in the morning with your guests, or making mimosas, or sleeping in! I recommend reading through the recipe and prepping as much as you can before you start. I find it much more fun, especially if you have guests around who are chatting about their golf game or their recent cruise.

<u>Ingredients</u>

4 oz. butter plus some for the pan
$^2/_3$ C firmly packed dark brown sugar
30-oz. canned crushed pineapple in juice, drained, retaining $^1/_3$ C juice
8 1-inch-thick slices sourdough French bread
3 large eggs
1 C milk
$^1/_2$ C half-and-half
$^1/_4$ t salt
$^1/_4$ t cinnamon
$^1/_4$ + t vanilla extract
$1^1/_2$ C toasted macadamia nuts, coarsely chopped
8 oz. mascarpone cheese, whipped with a little cream and 2 t powdered sugar
Extra powdered sugar to sprinkle on each serving

The night before, butter a 13 x 9 x 2-inch baking dish. (If you are using a loaf of bread that is extra-large in diameter, you may need to use a larger baking dish. Then, melt $^1/_4$ C butter in a saucepan over moderate heat and stir in the sugar until dissolved. Add the pineapple, stirring well to incorporate. Spread the pineapple mixture evenly in the bottom of the buttered baking dish.

Place the bread slices over the pineapple mixture, squeezing a little to make them fit.

In a bowl, whisk together the eggs, milk, half-and-half, reserved pineapple juice, salt, cinnamon, and vanilla extract (a little more than $^1/_4$ t, if you like it as much as I do).

Pour the egg mixture evenly over the bread. Cover with plastic wrap and refrigerate overnight.

The recipe continues.

In the morning, remove the baking dish from the refrigerator $^1/_2$ hour before baking. Preheat the oven to 400°. Bake the toast in the middle of the oven for 20 to 25 minutes, or until the bread is golden.

Serve one to two slices per person, depending on appetite. Carefully slip a spatula under all the pineapple and sauce and flip each piece of toast over onto the plate. You may need to use a spoon or fork to adjust the topping a little. Sprinkle with powdered sugar and serve with small bowls of macadamia nuts and whipped mascarpone at the table.

This makes a sweet French toast, so I add no topping or other sweetener. If you prefer something more, you can sprinkle with a little powdered sugar. I think it's lovely with just the raisins and candied fruit shining through.

Begin with panettone that has been sliced ¾-inch thick. (It is easier to slice when frozen, so I recommend that you begin with it frozen and slice it the night before. Place the slices in resealable storage bags or wrap with plastic wrap.

When ready to assemble, whisk 4 to 6 eggs with whole milk or half-and-half and a pinch of salt (more or less, depending on how many slices you are preparing). Melt some or half a stick of butter.

Have a griddle hot, but not too hot. The sugar in the panettone will burn quickly if the pan is too hot.

Dip slices of panettone in egg mixture and set on a plate before starting to cook. Spoon melted butter in small pools on the griddle, one before each slice is placed on the hot griddle.

Work rapidly so the butter doesn't brown. Cook until the panettone is golden-brown on one side and flip to cook the other side. Serve immediately and enjoy!

"Everything can have drama if it's done right.
Even a pancake."
—Julia Child

Flour, Eggs, Carrots, Apple, Dried Cherries. . .

Apple Carrot Muffins

I change the ingredients of this recipe every time I make these muffins, depending on what's in the pantry. Not everyone likes raisins, and I LOVE dried cherries. My husband doesn't like coconut.. So, whatever floats your boat (or is in your pantry)—go for it! Hope you like them.

<u>Ingredients</u>

2$\frac{1}{2}$ C all-purpose flour
1 t baking powder
1 t baking soda
$\frac{1}{2}$ t salt
$\frac{1}{2}$ t cinnamon
3–4 T mixed grains/seeds, such as wheat germ, chia seeds, flax (optional—I use)
1$\frac{1}{2}$ C shredded carrots (I sometimes add more)
1 large crispy apple (peeled, cored and shredded)
1 C vegetable oil
1$\frac{1}{2}$ C sugar
3 large eggs at room temperature (temp is important)
1 t vanilla extract
$\frac{1}{2}$ c pitted dried cherries (or raisins or prunes) (I soak them in warm water and then chop)
$\frac{1}{2}$ C shredded coconut (optional—I don't use)

Preheat oven to 400 degrees.

Dab a little shortening or butter in bottom of muffin tins and line with muffin paper (I sometimes end up with more than twelve with this recipe.)

Whisk together the flour, baking powder, baking soda, salt, cinnamon, and grains in a medium bowl. Combine carrots and apple in another bowl.

Beat the oil and sugar together with either a stand or hand mixer for *at least* 2 minutes. This is an important step, and I sometimes beat the mixture longer. Then add the eggs, one at a time, mixing well after each addition. The mixture will be thick.

With mixer on low speed add the flour mixture, alternating with the carrot/apple mixture, half at a time, just until incorporated. Then stir in whatever else you are adding, such as dried fruit or coconut.

Use a $\frac{1}{4}$ C scoop to fill the muffin cups and bake approximately 22 minutes. (Test doneness with a pick.) A clean pick depicts a completed bake, as you know. Let cool a few minutes in pan and then upend onto racks. Best if eaten fresh, but I do freeze my leftovers.

Breakfast Chiles Rellenos

I like to serve this as a side dish as part of a breakfast buffet, or bring it to a potluck. It can easily be prepared ahead of time.

<u>Ingredients</u>

3 4-oz. cans whole green Ortega chiles
1 C half-and-half
2 large eggs
8 oz. Monterey jack cheese, grated
8 oz. cheddar cheese, grated
1 C good tomato sauce for topping

Preheat oven to 375°.

Lightly oil a 1½-quart casserole dish.

Carefully split open the chiles and remove the seeds. Lay on paper towels to drain. Whisk the eggs with half-and-half until smooth.

Mix the two cheeses together, reserving ½ C of mixture for the topping.

To assemble the casserole, place one layer of chiles in bottom of oiled pan, then a layer of cheese, then egg mixture—alternating until all ingredients are used.

Spoon some tomato sauce on the top and sprinkle with reserved cheese.

Bake uncovered for 1 hour.

Lemon Pancakes

These are wonderful served with fresh berries. And, if you like, you can heat a cup of berries in the maple syrup for 2 or 3 minutes to serve over the pancakes for an extra treat!

<u>Ingredients</u>

2 C all-purpose flour
1 T sugar
1 t baking soda
1 t baking powder
$\frac{1}{2}$ t salt
2 large eggs, yolks and whites separated
$\frac{1}{2}$ C buttermilk
$1\frac{1}{4}$ C whole milk
2 t lemon zest
1 T lemon juice
1 t vanilla extract
4 T butter, melted, plus extra for the griddle
1 C maple syrup
1 C berries (blueberries are very nice—opt.)

In a large bowl, mix flour, sugar, baking soda, baking powder, and salt.

In a smaller bowl, whisk together the egg yolks, buttermilk, whole milk, lemon zest and juice, vanilla extract, and butter.

In a mixer on high speed, beat the egg whites until they form soft peaks. Gently stir the buttermilk mixture into the flour mixture just until blended. Gently fold in egg whites.

Preheat large griddle, if you have one, on medium heat over two burners. Otherwise, you can use a heavy skillet. Melt butter and spread with brush. When hot, pour $\frac{1}{4}$ C batter for each pancake and cook until golden on each side. Watch heat carefully and let second rise fluff up the pancake nicely. Serve with maple syrup.

Index

Made in the USA
Middletown, DE
01 December 2021

53848710R00097